THE ART OF LIVING ARTFULLY

LIVE AN

ARTFUL

LIFE

THOMAS NEEL

ISBN 978-1-7329937-0-9 (softcover)
ISBN 978-1-7329937-1-6 (eBook)

Chapter Illustrations and poems by Tom Neel
Cover and Interior design by Glen Edelstein

Live An Artful Life Inc
8908 Woodward Rd
Marshall, VA 20115
LiveAnArtfulLife.com

Live An Artful Life® is a registered trademark of Live An Artful Life Inc

I dedicate this book to my late mother Vivian.
A lively creative spirit, who always brought energy to a room.

CONTENTS

PREFACE   ix

INTRODUCTION   xiii

CHAPTER 1: *Live An Artful Life*   1

CHAPTER 2: *Lifestyle, Happiness, and Wellness*   13

CHAPTER 3: *Appreciation vs. Creation*   27

CHAPTER 4: *The Beauty Creativity Brings Us*   35

CHAPTER 5: *Your Creative Voice*   39

CHAPTER 6: *Action, Process, and Fulfillment*   51

CHAPTER 7: *Putting You In Your Artfulness - Emotion*   57

CHAPTER 8: *Overcoming Obstacles*   67

CHAPTER 9: *Being Resourceful, Problem Solving, Visual Awareness*   87

CHAPTER 10: *Learn and Practice by Doodling*   95

CHAPTER 11: *Artistic Productivity*   101

CHAPTER 12: *Your Perception of Success*   107

CHAPTER 13: *Improvement and Creative Longevity*   113

CHAPTER 14: *Ageless Artistry!*   121

CHAPTER 15: *Creating While Listening to Music or Books*   127

CHAPTER 16: *Some Artful Ways to Get Started*   133

CHAPTER 17: *Final Thoughts*   139

ACKNOWLEDGMENTS   143

ABOUT THE AUTHOR   145

PREFACE

WHERE ART BEGAN nearly 40,000 years ago as a form of communication, record keeping, and possibly early creative development, for me, art started as a way of creating things I dreamed about having. Serendipitously, it became my salvation—an escape to another world. My imagination was very active, and the artful world I gave myself to visit was as well. Art was quite therapeutic for me back at a time when entering therapy pretty much meant you were coo-coo.

You see, our home was a dysfunctional one. My father suffered from a rare enzyme disease called Alpha-1 antitrypsin deficiency, which essentially meant he was predisposed to die from emphysema whether he smoked or not. As such, he suffered a mild heart attack at age thirty-five, and didn't live past fifty-two. In the process, he lived a frustrated, often angry life. Call it tough family love, but it manifested itself at times with demeaning and violent repercussions. I both loved and feared him until I was sixteen, at which point I started standing up for myself. But my parents had separated and divorced by then.

This was during the 1970s, at a time when the overwhelming majority of poor marriages chose the path of living unhappily ever after. I went to a high school with 2,000 other students, yet I was the only one with divorced parents.

Creativity was a wonderful escape during these years, and fit well with my early development of an eager imagination. I had a passion for cars and car racing. Drawing and building model cars became a place not only of mental safety, but it also allowed me to enjoy myself in a world where time would drift away. It was developmental to both my brain and hand-eye coordination. And the model shows I entered at a young age taught me resourcefulness, goal setting, work ethic, skill advancement, and ways to achieve success.

So, despite the previously mentioned events, I was capable of at least some inner peace. I was most happy with the results of my creativity, which helped build my self-esteem. When my brain was engaged with my hands, and both were focused on drawing, building, or making something, I was in heaven.

During this fragile time, laced into the fabric of my life were two other hurtles. The first was a lazy eye, which was eventually corrected with glasses. The second was some level of dyslexia. It made standard forms of learning—especially reading—challenging, and some attention deficient was likely its willing partner.

It was creativity that came to my rescue again. Oddly, this time in the form of writing. While I was damn near failing English class in high school, I was excelling in journalism class and was writing for the school paper. I attributed much of this to a bad English teacher and an amazing journalism teacher. One couldn't see the forest through the trees, and the other was a visionary.

Miss Heidelberger (Robert E. Peary High School) saw in me what just about no other human on the planet could. She gave me confidence and challenges. I would say she even championed me and validated my creative spirit. This came at a time when I needed someone—anyone—to do so. It felt great, and I honestly feel a deep sense of gratitude to her to this day.

Fortune would have it that neither my brother nor I would have my father's unhealthy gene. I wore glasses from the seventh to the ninth grade to correct my lazy eye problem. By the time I graduated high school I had found my dyslexia had given me an interesting *spatial* awareness. It's an advantage that I use to this day, even though typing is still a bit of a battlefield. But it is my artfulness that has given me a healthy and very blessed life. I chased my love of cars through every facet, but my life's love came at age thirty-two when I dropped cars as a career to immerse myself in creativity. It was indeed my calling. Over three decades later, my professional career as an artist has given me so much joy; and no, I haven't starved. But learning to *live an artful life* has not been just about being an artist. It has also been a type of currency in my life. An asset as crucial as any dollar I have ever received.

To *live an artful life* is about using your imagination and creative spirit to cheer on the champion within you. It's home plate in that baseball diamond of a world we live in.

We all have to run those bases, but you don't want to just run in endless circles without life having value and scoring some home runs!

Not everyone is meant to be an artist in the literal sense. But this does not mean the benefits of an artful life are elusive, and you should know that we all are creative. I know this to be true, even if you have been told differently.

Many times in my life as an artist, I've had someone tell me, "I can't draw a straight line with a ruler." To which I always say, "Let's just get a ruler and get you past that right now." In return they'll say they're kidding and ask if I know what they mean.

No, I honestly don't. Any time someone comes to me trying to imply they are not creative, I've proven every one of them wrong in a matter of minutes. The point here is that we all are creative in some way. And it's been my experience that properly developed creativity brings out an inner voice—one which always has something to say. In doing so, it releases stress, promotes self-improvement, and gives you confidence. Oh, and best of all, it's fun too!

This book is intended for people of all generations. It is meant to help you possibly find, validate, or share how creativity and living artfully can be an essential part of the human experience we call life. I wrote this book to give you a second chance to tap into your youth, to feel good, and to promote an enjoyable, carefree life. Win, win, win.

INTRODUCTION

IT WAS 1988. The movie *Rain Man* was a hit, the Dow Jones Industrial hovered around 2,000, and George Herbert Walker Bush was elected president. Oh, and I became a working artist. Thirty years later, I'm so happy that I had the foresight as a younger man to go for it. To have had the understanding that this *is* the actual play, not the rehearsal.

Perhaps the reminder had been of my father, who passed away in 1979 when both he and I were too young. He had already been gone more than a handful of years as I was transitioning to my career in art. I was left to learn on my own that life may bring you opportunity, but you must bring to that life the actions, decisions, and intentions it needs to make you whole. So, I *decided* to become an artist. I took *action* and *intended* on being successful. It wasn't easy, but it was satisfying, as I had re-entered an inspirited life of self-expression and creativity, where my brain and hands would work as a team.

This book is a philosophical extension of the life I have been living ever since. One which was born out of my childhood love of imagination, and learning of its beneficial power to help the mind and body in many ways. Chief among them is with lowered stress through having a *carefree* attitude. You will notice that I did not say careful or careless. Being carefree allows for freedom, discovery, and happiness while still also being accountable for one's actions, intentions, and responsibilities.

We live in a demanding, non-stop 24/7 world today. As if we are all a bunch of shooting stars—bright for a moment but headed for burnout. We focus on monetary needs and achievements, often with our noses planted into some device rather than paying attention to our family, friends, or, as you will come to find in this book, ourselves. Our inner creative voice sounds either like a suffocating whisper or a scream of starvation. Either way, we often ignore it while racing around trying to keep up, yet often in a deep rut.

If this sounds like you, then hello! I'm happy to meet you, and hopefully my words will offer a new or validating direction. At the very least, I hope you see options for and within yourself. I wrote this book over a reasonable period, but I didn't want it to be about page count or wordiness. Time is important to us all, and I respect and appreciate yours!

The first five chapters offer the philosophy and tools of understanding. The next five chapters are about action, and the last five or so chapters provide an additional understanding of goals and final thoughts. It is a book I feel most can read and benefit from pretty quickly. Afterward, you can use my highlighted statements found in each chapter to quickly go back through the book at any time as a refresher. If anything jumps out at you as a possible problem area, you can then easily re-read that section to get back on track. Think of it like being in an airport and hitting the people mover! If you find this book helpful (and I sincerely hope you do), I feel these quick refreshers will help you adopt it as a gratifying lifestyle.

I also believe in the laws of attraction and visualization, and that your intentions are a very powerful tool. It seems no sooner than I put my mind to this artistic task that serendipity brought me a teammate in the way of my wife-to-be, Linda. On her own journey for happiness, Linda had left her first career in IT, moved east from Colorado and opened Leesburg, Virginia's first art gallery. I met Linda while visiting the gallery and we hit it off instantly. Linda ended up representing my paintings in the gallery, and it became much like a launching pad with Linda as the fuel and me as the rocket! 3-2-1- Blast off!

A word or two about wellness. I am not a doctor or scientist, but I do reasonably believe myself to be as much a creative behavior observer as anyone. I've had an endless amount of conversation with both creative types and non-creative types about creativity.

In a gallery setting, when people find out I'm an artist, they quickly open up about wishing they had time to create, or all the reasons why they are not creative, or how they used to be and would still love to be, but can't. I have been a local support system for anyone who I could help move that ball forward. I have done this through my monthly newspaper article of ten years, "The Artist's Perspective," through our weekly blog and creative and inspiring content website called *Live An Artful Life,* and through public speaking.

For what it's worth, as I write this I am sixty-three years of age, with barely a gray hair, but hey, there's only so much of it left! I don't take any prescription drugs and see the doctor once a year for a physical. Is this because of being an artist? Perhaps not entirely, but I feel very strongly that my artful lifestyle supports my health, and the same should be said of Linda.

I've been an artist for thirty years. Thirty years has its summits; peaks that give you a more favorable perspective of the valleys one must experience in life and with any career covering three decades. One of the most rewarding parts of my business was choosing to be commissioned as an artist. To focus on customer service and allowing my clients to take me down paths I might not otherwise explore. This has also allowed me to experience the celebratory feelings of others.

When I paint a painting celebrating a person's 50th-year retirement or a couple's 45th wedding anniversary, I am frankly honored. Then there are also those wonderful relationships and friendships that blossom out of such requests. Other relationships are born out of philanthropy. As an example, working with golf legend Jack Nicklaus and his lovely wife Barbara over the years has allowed my art to raise tens of thousands in much-needed funds for their Nicklaus Children's Health Care Foundation.

Fortunately, there have been informative lessons learned along the way. Allow me to share a few. An investment counselor once asked me, "When do you see yourself retiring?" My answer, "Retire? I already do what people do when they retire." In short, find something you love, and it won't be work. Also, you know that old saying, *starving artist*? Well, I never have. Art has been my passion, and my lifestyle.

The past thirty years have been a magical time of creative expression, low stress, and happiness. It's not too much to ask of your life. And to every young person, I say just three things. Don't smoke—it will ruin your life. Be passionate about your intentions, and let happiness guide you. That doesn't mean you don't have to apply yourself to your goals. It just means find goals worth passionately pursuing. Oh yes, and live in an area that fuels your soul. One that beckons you to do as much for it, as it does for you! Then *Live An Artful Life*. Your *artful life!*

LIVE AN **ARTFUL** LIFE

CHAPTER I

Live An Artful Life

You deserve the life,
An artful life can bring.
Filled to the brim with gratitude,
And surrounded by creative things!

I HAVE BEEN CREATIVE all my life. For me, artfulness is one of life's greatest gifts. It has not only allowed me to voice myself in amazing ways and with an abundance of freedom, but my art has also allowed me to truly touch others in positive ways. This artfulness has become a way of life. A lifestyle which I believe has contributed to my happiness, my health, and yes, even my ability to inspire others around me. Creativity, by its magnificent nature, also allows you to be open to options, problem solving, and experimentation. It gives you tools to experiment or attempt.

Sometimes people don't even try. Instead, they just exist, often feeling optionless in the process, and no one who loves life should feel optionless!

This artfulness comes from active inspiration.

This artfulness or creativity also opens you to a world where you can express yourself in boundless ways as if you are creating a new language—the language of you! This artfulness comes from *active inspiration.* I believe we all can and should be inspired, and as often as possible, even if we are not ultimately creative in the artistic sense of the word. The trouble is, many of us don't tap into the inspiration around us or even attempt to activate our imaginations. Inspiration and imagination are vital to being artful. It's just a matter of opening your mind up to an inspired you. So, you might be asking why? Or, where will this active inspiration get me? To that I say, you may find a greater understanding of yourself or even a whole new you!

Imagine for a moment being in the grocery store with a choice in front of you. That choice is merely to buy peanut butter. Pick the one you want and forget the brand itself: focus on the label and what may have attracted you to it. Let's go a little deeper—will you choose smooth or chunky? Why? Now, someone in peanut butter land has given a whole lot of thought toward trying to figure out the personal complexities of texture or the lack of it, and you can bet this simple choice says something about the inner you.

I see this one decision as not only a preference, but an artistic choice as well. The decision between smooth and chunky is not a taste-driven thing as much as it is a texture-driven one. And texture, or the lack of it, is a personal characteristic that says something about you. Some people like their lives to go smoothly, while others like a little crunch, or challenge, or even competition to sneak in there. That texture may find its way into other parts of your life too, especially an artistic one.

If you have to drive someplace, do you like the radio on or

off? This decision is about sound or silence. Similarly, there are those who sleep with the TV on. If you don't, you may wonder, how can anyone relax enough to sleep with all that noise? And they may wonder how you can sleep without it! Perhaps people who do this simply want company, and in a creative world they may wish for or need collaboration. Being aware of these habits though, is a form of active inspiration, empowering you with a greater knowledge of what drives you, what makes you tick and if creative, artistically floats your boat.

So, while I could go on with many more examples, allow me to ask this about your life in general: Do you live your life in color, or in black & white? Is it dark or light, highlighted or in the shadows? Filled with contrast and hard edges, or soft? Is it vertical or horizontal? Is it two dimensional or three dimensional? Is it real or an abstract illusion, one that can't be touched or one that touches you? Is it blank space ready to be filled, or filled space ready to be erased? Is your life smooth or textured? One with words to be said, or words to be sung? Is it amplified or acoustic? In pitch, in harmony, or out of tune? Is it audible or visual, tall or short, wide or narrow, modern, traditional or even antique? These artistic observations are how my brain visualizes life. As an artist, I speak through creative expression, and I think you likely do too, on some level.

> *Artistic observations are how my brain visualizes life.*

If you take those questions above and convert them into personal characteristics, all will likely apply to you in some manner of your happiness and ultimately your wellness too. One person's pleasure can be another person's torture. But at the very least, all of these artistic characteristics are, in a sense, knobs of adjustments in you and it's likely some are compromises you live with right now.

For instance, you may desire a modern home, but perhaps you live in a traditional one because of the region you live in for work. So here's one decision: *modern, traditional or antique.* Or suppose you live in a three-story townhouse but desire one-floor living. Here's another decision: *vertical or horizontal.* Or maybe you work in an environment of gray walls but excel in a place of color: *color, black & white, or gray.* You may be single and want to have a partner. On the other hand, maybe you are ready for divorce: *blank space ready to be filled, or filled space ready to be emptied.* Or maybe your life is filled with continuous noise, and all you want is some silence. Or perhaps it's classical, and you just want to rock & roll: *amplified or acoustic.*

You see, any of these artistic expressions can be converted to real life because regardless of how artistry expresses itself, it is always the artist's inner self at play. You might also notice that artists very often come in two flavors, much like everyone else, but often more extreme versions. They are either solitary creatures, introverted and shy, or zany, colorful, even flamboyant individuals who don't just express themselves with art, rather, they *are* art!

I think many of us would love to allow ourselves that ultimate freedom. The kind that requires a societal sense of courage—that non-conforming, attention-grabbing bravery. Perhaps not, but I believe the world tends to look at artists as people capable of baring their souls through their artwork. This is how living an artful life can feel. Life is a journey, and living artfully can make this journey more fun, more interesting, even more bearable for some.

> *Life is a journey, and living artfully can make this journey more fun, more interesting, even more bearable for some.*

To better understand "the tree" I'm presenting here, it's easier to have a look at its roots first. Let's look closer at the words *Live An Artful Life*. **Live** - *Not to just exist, not just the time between birth and death, but to live and experience life*. **Artful** - *Showing creative skill, cleverness or taste*. **Life** - *Again, not to just exist, but to possess the capacity to grow*! In other words, to *Live An Artful Life* is to grow through experiencing the power of creativity, the freedom of imagination, and sharing your inspiration with others. It's not only knowing art exists, it's allowing artful things to live within and around you. For it to inspire you and bring you joy—to be another language or voice.

The phrase, *stop and smell the roses* is a classic example of how to live an artful life. So please allow me to ask a simple yet complex question: Are you happy? This one question is complex in that it may conjure up feelings as to what the true definition of happiness is for you. So, I would like you to pause for a moment and really give it some thought and then ask yourself, *Am I happy?*

Now, if you have a big old grin on your face after shouting out a resounding yes, then you know the world is your studio! But if you're feeling a bit less enthusiastic about your smile factor, please read on. And if you're saying true happiness is a fantasy, just three more paragraphs, please.

Live an artful life. These four words may sound like a fantasy, and that's a great place to begin. Because fantasy is something you imagine, often thinking of it as a better or more exciting world than the reality of life you are living. So often, we associate a world of fantasy with the innocence and naiveté of a child. But that doesn't stop many of us from fantasizing about winning the lottery and imagining a life of wealth. Fantasy is by no means a bad thing, and it certainly has a real and essential place in our reality.

Look no further than the success of the *Star Wars* series to prove the world loves fantasy. Then there's *Harry Potter*, *Lord of the Rings*, or anything made by Pixar. Reach deeper into your youth and name your favorite Disney movie. How about *The Nutcracker,* or great books like *Treasure Island*, *Robin Hood* or *Alice in Wonderland*?

And when I say Christmas, do you think of a jolly big guy in a red suit with a bushy white beard, maybe with a sleigh and reindeer? Of course, you do. It's all fantasy, but here's the key: while it all may be fantasy, it is a fantastic and healthy by-product of someone else's imagination, which now has a perception or level of reality to you, and your life is way better for it.

For any fantasy to be formed and visualized, it must be conceived from some form of one's reality. Take *Alice in Wonderland*, which depicts a young girl chasing a rabbit. That could be a reality. Becoming smaller and larger by eating (too much) cake? Well, that could be a reality too! But the scale in which Alice changes, of course, is a fantasy. There is, however, enough reality in the story to help you wrap your arms around it, so on we go along with this priceless and wonderful journey.

I have spent most of my adult life as a professional artist. From one point of view, one would say I have made my living through paintings. Though true, this is a narrow, monetary viewpoint. The broader truth is, I bring reality to the imaginations of everyday people and thus, I bring them pleasure. If they love the things I paint, it is because I am creating that which they visually or emotionally desire. That which provokes thought, knowledge, enjoyment, tranquility, passion, or intrigue.

Art is primarily an emotional illusion, a rendering of the human experience. And without question, it enhances one's reality. It doesn't matter whether it comes in the form of a painting or a song, written words, a theatrical performance, or dance. Or from a book or film, one which includes a young girl's escapades while chasing a rabbit down its hole.

*Your life is **your** life, right?*

As an artist, I am a practitioner of visualization. I believe it is one of the most effective ways of getting you where you want to be. I will talk about visualization in the coming chapters, but most important for now is the control it gives you. Visualization allows you to open your roadmap and chart your course. It's like having an internal navigation system. You don't have to share it or be ashamed of how grand your thoughts, ideas, desires, or goals are. You just need to close your eyes and imagine it.

Your life is *your* life, right? It sounds so simple, doesn't it? But now ask yourself; is your life really *yours*? I mean, if it is yours, meaning you own it, and it's truly yours to do what you wish with it, are you doing what you really want with *your* life? Are you the authentic you?

Earlier, I asked if you were happy because so often we live a job, not a life. We confuse the two. We become what we do. Don't get me wrong, many love what they do, but they almost always are so much more than what they do. Still others dislike what they do and yet, they not only keep doing it, they do it for so long that once retired, they do not even know who they are. They just become a retired whatever-they-were.

The worst time for this happens right before you retire. It's a transitional time which is both a good and bad time to be finding yourself. Part of you sees the future, but the part of you that has become what you've done for a living all those years holds on to that identity and has trouble letting go of the position, status, and pay you've worked a lifetime to achieve. You find yourself trying to find yourself. This is where you need to have a belief in your interests past work and see yourself as much more than what you've been doing for a living. If you have no hobbies or other interests, allow yourself to explore the self-expressive inner you. Give creativity a try and by all means allow yourself to be carefree. You've worked your life away to be able to do so.

If you are young, finding yourself is often even harder. To the young I say, please don't lose your youthful creative spirit in the aging process. It's one thing to become an adult and to accept your responsibilities, but not at the cost of losing your youthfulness. You know, that playful risk of living, learning and loving life.

In my life as an artist, I've met so many good people, young and old. I can see the happiness on their faces when they find out I'm an artist. It's as if they are meeting not only what they perceive as a happy person, but someone doing what they want with their life. Often they open up to me about their creative desires, while in the same breath, speak of their endless responsibilities. In life, there is no shortage of responsibilities—this is for sure, even for an artist! Regardless though, I encourage everyone to make time for that creative person inside.

You do not have to be a specific age, creative in the artistic sense, or financially sound in order to live an artful life. Simply put, to *live an artful life* is to foster and feed imagination so as to make one's reality brighter, happier, and more exciting and full. It matters not if you are creative or the creator who brings that imagination to a reality of sorts. However, if active creativity is not your path right now, be the one who surrounds yourself with the creativity of others.

To live an artful life is to immerse yourself in something other than the mundane and enjoy life to its fullest through a world of visionary exploration.

To *live an artful life* is not necessarily to bust out of your comfort circle with wild abandonment. Though if that's what it takes, everyone's door and key looks different. More so, to *live an artful life* is to enjoy any subconscious circle you've created. To *live an artful life* is to immerse yourself in something other than the mundane and enjoy life to its fullest through a world of visionary exploration. Make it your lifestyle. The benefits are real, and emotion is your willing guide. Never ask yourself, *is this all there is?* Because there's not only more, there's way more! Life should be thought of as an account with a high rate of return in abundance for those who invest in themselves.

CHAPTER 2

Lifestyle, Happiness, and Wellness

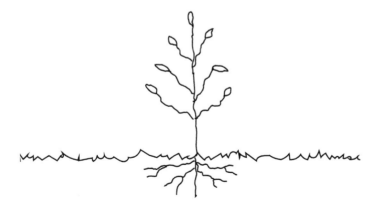

Your life in style,
Is little to nothing without a smile.
And then there's wellness too!
A healthy life is a healthy you!

LIFE CAN BE MUNDANE if you allow it to be. The good thing is, it doesn't have to be. It just takes one simple change to truly live artfully, and that's *being carefree.*

Sound too simple? Are you begging for complexity? Okay, try this: *Being carefree, as much as you'll allow yourself within your realm of endless responsibilities to family, friends, work, and your budget.* Does that sound better? I didn't think so. Let's not cloud simplicity in complexity for no reason.

Carefree doesn't mean being reckless and not caring about anything. The essence of the word carefree is happiness. Is there anything more important than happiness? Being unhappy is stressful and stress makes you sick, so I don't think so. Being happy is the essence of feeling great about life. Feeling great about who you are as a person, your family and friends, your social interactions in general, and with humanity overall. There is nothing in this world better than feeling happy and making others feel happy, which in return, almost always leads to more of your own happiness! Carefree is not careless. Quite literally, it's anything but.

After all, a great life is not measured by how old you can become, it's measured in how young you feel while aging.

Still, happiness can mean different things to different people. Blanket happiness—happiness that covers everything—is quite an achievement. It requires a sincere positive outlook on life. Which, by the way, is proven not only to help wellness and longevity, but also the quality of life. After all, a great life is not measured by how old you can become, it's measured in how young you feel while aging.

It's well documented that the majority of centennials sight a positive outlook on life as their secret to longevity. For some people, happiness may only be about good health. For others, it is seeing your family do well, and yet for others, it may be having great wealth. For me, creative happiness ranks very high in the overall happiness scale. For the act of creating means I am highly engaged with my mind, soul, and body.

When you leave the world with something interesting in return for an interesting life, you are being productive. Creativity is a form of contribution for society's thought and entertainment, and it's a process in personal growth unlike almost anything else you can find. It is also one of the purest forms of freedom. Because in a sense, it allows you to make anything your mind can think up as possible.

Freedom of creative expression is as human a right and pleasure as there could ever be, and when it's taken away, you only find unhappiness in its place.

Freedom knows happiness. Just try living without it. You won't easily find an artful life there. There is no freer place than the mind, and no better way to express your freedom than through art or the joy of being artful. Even free speech is censored to a large degree. But there are no art police, there are no rules and regulations, no forms to fill out. Freedom of creative expression is as human a right and pleasure as there could ever be, and when it's taken away, you only find unhappiness in its place.

Show me a country that condemns the free-thinking of its artists and I will show you a place of unhappiness and suppression. Look to places around the world where governments control artists and radicals are destroying artifacts, to experience the polar opposite of the theory behind the words *live an artful life*. Artistry should be celebrated every day and society as a whole will always be better for it.

Remember that creative expression may certainly be your want, willingness, and enthusiasm, but just surrounding yourself with the creative expression of others is of great benefit as well. For example, listening to music, while reading a book, next to a painting, beside a sculpture, in a handmade chair, is its own form of creative expression and is most certainly *living an artful life*. As is wearing clothes with color, texture, and design, cooking with a visual touch, giving something handmade as a gift, doing something spontaneously, or even contributing to an uplifting social media message.

Being responsible to the point of suppressing your spirit is a recipe for disaster and leads to underlying stress.

So being carefree should never be looked at as being irresponsible. In fact, just the opposite. Being carefree is simply about you living life in living color, not putting off the adventures in life for a future of uncertainty and unrealized outcomes while being embroiled in self-inflicted responsibility.

Being responsible can be a very good thing. Being responsible to the point of suppressing your spirit is a recipe for disaster and leads to underlying stress, which certainly is not healthy and therefore, it can be said that this is a lack of responsibility in the first place. Take care of you and you can take care of others. But burn your inner house down and the cinders left can't help shelter a soul, especially yours!

Let me give a few real-life examples of this: my wife Linda and I have owned a couple of art galleries. One day, a husband and wife came in and began looking around. He looked very closely at several of my paintings, just inches away, as only an artist would. Art lovers look at paintings, but artists look at how paintings are painted. So they get close up in order to see brush strokes, how layers are applied, etc.

In time, he found out I am the artist who painted the paintings he was inspecting, and a great conversation began. This soon led me to find out he was both a professional analyst and an amateur artist. I don't say amateur because of a lack of talent; I say it because it was not his profession. He showed me his work via his smartphone, an in reality, he was quite a good painter and could have been a professional if he wished. But he was decades into a full-time career.

Our conversation allowed me to know his years of dedication to his career made him feel a sense of responsibility to it, even though I felt he could retire. Even if painting was now his priority, he was having trouble wondering whether he should pursue it, if the timing was right, whether he was good enough, and even whether he deserved it. He didn't know how to go about getting started and in short, he didn't have that carefree feeling. His art seemed to be both a joy and a burden to him. Why? Because his responsibility was to his job. And to leave that behind, even though he had spent decades doing everything to allow him to do so, seemed irresponsible.

The career—a good thing. Devotion to doing a good job—a very good thing. A long career making a valuable contribution to an employer and one's responsibilities—a great thing. Not knowing how to stop, however, is not a good thing. Not being able to say you're an artist when you are quite good at self-expression and have honed a talent— definitely not a good thing.

In this example, this gentleman had been painting as a hobby for many years. If asked what he does, his correct answer should be that he's an analyst and also an artist. If he had been telling himself and others this, I feel he would be more carefree to act on the second chapter of his life. That is being responsible to yourself. He loves painting, he's dedicated years to it, and his devotion has netted him genuinely favorable results. But his job is who he feels he is, and so it has now become the leash that's taking him for a walk.

To be fair, I do not think this man was dreadfully unhappy. I will say though, I don't think he was honestly happy either and definitely not carefree. My advice was to go part-time; be a consultant, but don't miss the opportunity to do what you really love. It was apparent that his schedule limited his creativity a lot. He desperately wanted to share his art with me, and he did. He felt a need to do so and I was happy we found that common ground. If I hadn't been an artist, he couldn't have been himself and opened up to me. He would have just been an analyst that day, looking at art, rather than someone who, in reality, felt he was also a gifted artist.

> *One thing I can promise you is the meaning of life is not death.*

When we are busy climbing the ladder while we're young and providing for ourselves and family, we often confuse our results-driven career growth with happiness. For some, it actually may be a derivative of happiness. But there's that old saying about being on your deathbed and not saying, *I wish I could have worked another day*. Doing what you love is not work. Don't let your last day be the day you figure life out.

Many ponder the meaning of life. One thing I can promise you is the meaning of life is not death. I say balance it all out; there's no sense in waiting to the final curtain call to deliver that beautiful, carefree performance, especially when you can have a life full of it without the drama!

Life should never be thought of as a race either. Everyone that knows racing knows two things; exactly where the finish line is and how far you have to go or how much time you have to get there. Most of us don't know this about life. If you do know, and your life is now a race, it's a race with time. For most of us though, life is not a set time and it sure as hell should not be a race.

You may say life is set by destiny, but I'll say as an example, that no one is destined to smoke cigarettes. That's a choice statistically proven to shorten life, as does stress.

So going back to the race analogy above, the race is timed, but the smoker has made a personal choice to crash before the race is over. To likely not only end his or her race early, but to go to great personal expense in doing so. Smoking better damn sight be fun for you then, but I have never spoken to anyone who said it was, including both of my now deceased parents.

Carefreeness is about happiness; carefulness is the opposite, and carelessness lacks intelligence.

This is not about smoking though—this is about choices. Smoking may seem carefree, but it's NOT. It's an addiction and utterly careless. So, *carefreeness* is about happiness, freedom of thought, expanding your comfort circle, knowing more than one type of person, knowing more than one type of you, exploring the less obvious, not caring about stereotypes, having fun and living life. *Carefulness* is the opposite. It's not allowing yourself to explore. And *carelessness?* Well, carelessness just lacks intelligence.

I have a friend who became very successful at quite a young age. By all accounts, he was a successful entrepreneur and businessman. Seeing his abundance of outward signs of wealth would have most certainly told anyone he was hugely successful. The mansion, exotic cars, helicopter, and jet—you get the picture. He came from nothing and became a self-made millionaire, but this luxury did come at a stressful price.

As the years passed, he traded that stressful, demanding life in for a new one. He could have kept going for it. Instead, he stopped and turned back to his creative passions—a love of jazz, the thought of being a musician again as he once was in college, and a love of dance and live performance. Today, he plays jazz music professionally, and he heads up a non-profit dance company. Both require business skills, so his talent in this area is not at all lost. But it's not the principal driver of his life either; creativity is. He lives as artful a life as anyone I know, yet his background was math.

Interestingly, he was recently offered a CEO position at a company. The kind of job any ladder climber would dream of. When I asked his decision, he told me, "What? and give up the best years of my life?" The answer was no! Most of us are just too mentally insecure to walk away from money, even past our true need for it. Hey, money is a good thing, unless it's also a prison. Sometimes we have to be true to ourselves in what we are chasing.

So, I asked my friend this; when did you know you were successful? The answer could have been such a cliché of sorts: when I bought my Ferrari, or when I built my big house. But no, he gave the most beautiful answer. He said he didn't know until he retired from business and started living well below his means. He would explain that while he had amassed great wealth and all of the outward signs of it, he was too busy caring about the scorecard to even understand exactly what he had. Therefore, he was missing what was important to the true quality of his own life.

While my friend is still a very wealthy person, he doesn't measure his life in things, but rather experiences. His thirst to make money simply to have more, has been replaced with a more authentic form of happiness, like making music with other musicians. I would be willing to bet he would tell you that being accepted as a musician by other musicians is way, way more fulfilling than his peer relationships in the business world, despite the fact he was highly regarded and in many ways still is. But the musicians he plays with could care less about that. They care if he's passionate about jazz and has the chops. That *cred* means everything to him.

I once started a conversation with a woman who was looking around our gallery. The discussion, which began with art, soon became one about life. She was not really at that downsizing age, yet downsizing is what she had just done. I didn't pry as to the catalyst for this change in her life, but she had sold her house and in the process, almost everything in it as well. She moved into a modest-sized city apartment, bringing only a dozen or so boxes. Everything else was now in her past.

Some might feel imprisoned by such a move, but she happily described it as freeing. You could tell that her search for things to bring into her new life and home was very much about quality and meaningfulness, not just stuff and clutter. First, she was looking for the right art to capture the right feel. That emotional connection. She wanted things that were handmade, ones with feeling and meaning. I didn't know the other version of this person, but the new version was intent on *living an artful life* and living carefree. She radiated a stress-free happiness that was a pleasure to see.

To *live an artful life,* one doesn't need to have a radical lifestyle change. But these examples show people who have happily embraced it. Their happiness in doing so was life-changing.

A far less radical case might be the scarf show my wife Linda put on at our gallery. Now mind you, scarves, like coffee, are not a new thing. In any event, Linda's event was not just with any scarves, but rather featured 200 handmade and very creative scarves. A scarf is not only a very functional wearable accessory; it can be stylish and artful as well! The fun, *live an artful life* part of this show though, was a special night to participate and learn twenty-five different ways to tie your scarf. Almost nothing could be more *live an artful life* by nature.

Seeing and feeling an abundance of handmade things by true artisans, in an artful environment, with like-minded people, while learning something new is uplifting, gives you a new look, and a new feel creates a new you. Small things can add up to significant change. In this case, it's not merely about buying something; it is about the joy, experience, immersion, and interaction into creative expression. Participants, in this case, all women, felt a bond. One where the creativity of others brought real happiness. Learning something stylish and new was done in a very non-pressured, carefree and supportive way. I viewed it as if they were on a mini-vacation.

> *To live an artful life, you need to refocus on the greatness around you.*

In the end, without health where would we be? Words like *lifestyle* get quickly replaced with words like *quality of life*. But the wellness factors which come from happiness cannot be overlooked. We live at a time in our civilization where we're blessed with abundant food sources, shelter, hospitals, communication and even entertainment. Yet, we seem to be stressfully pounded by media alarmists, endless advertising and political rhetoric that make the world seem far worse than it is. So often, we, find ways to talk about things like the weather while looking down at our smart-phones rather than up at the sky. All the while letting the truly interesting things in life pass us by.

To *live an artful life,* you need to refocus on the greatness around you. It's okay to talk about the weather, but include that glorious sunrise you saw this morning. Don't just talk about the cold, talk about the delicious soup you made to keep warm. And by all means, don't just eat food, taste it. Savor it, discover its ingredients in each bite. These are healthy things to do. They are stress relievers and if you don't have time for such things, well then, ask yourself if you are happy about that. Or if you really ever will be? If you are happy, then you are living the life you wish to. On the other hand, if you say, *of course I'm not happy*, then stress is trying to be your friend and trust me, stress doesn't play fair. It's a far less than favorable life ingredient. There is no better day than today for a proper self-appraisal. A time in which you can take stock in yourself, your family and those around you.

All of us should feel a sense of place, not captured by where we are. We all should have an interest in what we do, rather than merely being bound by its monetary rewards. We all should be immersed in the present and fundamentally aware of the gift our life is, not locked in the phrase, *one day I'm going to…??* You must make sure that elusive *one day* you are in search of is not so very distant and without clarity. Live artfully today! Live an artful life.

CHAPTER 3

Appreciation vs. Creation

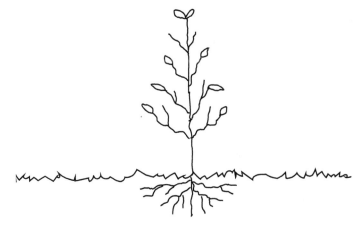

To Live An Artful Life,
All you have to do,
Is appreciate artful things,
But you can also make them too!

I HOPE THERE ARE some who read this book and find the *live an artful life* philosophy helpful, but who also do so while having no intention of being creative, as in wanting to become an artist in the literal sense of the word. Don't get me wrong, if that is what eventually happens or if you are already an artist and have turned to this book as a further source of inspiration and learning, that's great. But being or becoming an artist isn't necessary to realize the benefits of this lifestyle. A healthy *appreciation* for creativity is just as important as an active one and in many ways, maybe even more so for some. But even if you never intend to be an artist, a real sense of artistry can still live within you, and the chapters about actively being creative are therefore also important.

To live an artful life is to have a deep sense of how creativity works through you and around you, its process and even the obstacles.

To *live an artful life* is to have a deep sense of how creativity works through you and around you, its process and even the obstacles. This is not only true in a personal sense, but can easily fit a business sense as well. Creativity is much like a wave coming ashore. It rises out of a dynamic sea as an inspired thought or concept visualization. This is an exciting time in the creative cycle. You have an idea! But as previously mentioned, creativity itself is not an idea. Rather it is an action, or bringing an idea to reality, and as that wave comes to shore, it needs to build momentum before eventually crashing on the beach! As we know all too well though, some people love riding the wave, and some enjoy walking the beach, yet both have an appreciation for the sea. There's nothing wrong with walking the beach, feeling the sand between your toes, watching the waves crash in. You can still appreciate and enjoy those who ride them.

Creativity also comes in so many forms, and heightened creativity can sometimes even arise at different periods of a person's life. Being an artist is about creating something. It is about taking an idea and bringing it to reality through some form of self or collaborative expression. But where would creativity be without those with an appreciation for it in the first place? Art is simply a form of communication, a voice, and it really does want to communicate or speak to someone once it enters the world.

All art has something to say, and to those who feel you are either not creative or who do not wish to be creative at this point in your lives, no worries. You too can just as easily *live an artful life* and emotionally communicate with the creative voices of others who communicate through art. Sometimes you may even feel you must rob yourself of your personal feelings or emotions when seeing art. This, out of respect for the artist who created the work. It doesn't have to be this way.

The art appreciator has a full right to find or identify with their own story in every piece of art they see or hear. The words to a song can become your own story regardless of who wrote them. The actual act of creativity is by no means a prerequisite for any person's appreciation of art. Being inspired by creativity is! My guess is in adopting an artful lifestyle, some creative mojo will likely appear or rub off on you. Watch out. It might cozy up to the inner you!

> *To live an artful life is to simply have an artful attitude.*

It is worth mentioning to both the creator and the appreciator; if you have one person who takes a painting class every couple of weeks and another person who enjoys regular museum visits, gallery openings, live performances and perhaps even better, art collecting, make no mistake, both are *living an artful life*, and I would say quite equally. But possibly the second person is living a fuller one because their consumption is a broader enlightenment rather than simply a self-expressive one. In other words, art appreciation is just as important as artistic creation. To *live an artful life* is to simply have an artful attitude, an artful curiosity, become a sponge for artistic inspiration and realize that life without outward artistic expression would be much less of a life. Less fun, less full.

I'm sure you have visited someone's home and found it to have a more than average artistic flair and you know that the owner or owners are not what you would call artists. If that sense of artistry or decorative talent is of their own making, one might say that they are artists in a sense and their home is their canvas, their form of creative expression. This may even be you!

Some people have an eye for design, right? But you may be asking, were they born that way? Listen, we all are born with some advantages and disadvantages, likes and dislikes. Those born with that sense of flair or artistry though, are just more likely to be passionate to learn more about what they like.

At a young age if your thing is sports, you will do as much of it as you can, and as you do more, you get better and better. No one is born a tennis pro, but clearly, we are born with some brain wiring in place that helps us with life, that makes us different from others, and sets a path of discovery and self-improvement. By no means does it mean other things can't be learned. Of course, they can, and trust me now, you can learn to live more artfully. This I know.

We make creative decisions from the time we wake up every morning. We choose what to eat, which has at least something to do with how tasty our meal looks. We dress ourselves, matching colors and designs, most of which has to do with how we look. We then might get into our car to head to work in a car that reflects our choice in its size, shape, lines, and color. These are all artful decisions. We make many other artful decisions and creative choices during the day.

The key to all of this is understanding that we do make these decisions and largely based on those things I've mentioned, like whether your life is in color, black and white or gray, et cetera.

What color is your car, and why? What color lipstick do you use, and why? What predominant color is found in your closet? Why? Do you have a house with colored siding or brick, or perhaps it has some stone, maybe it's traditional or perhaps it's modern?

Once you think about your life in the context of these choices, it becomes a support system to living a much more artful life and gives you a great sense of you, thus making it easier to create a better, happier you. Inspiration comes from life around us, but our appreciation for artfulness in life must eventually come from within ourselves.

Once you think about it a little, it allows you to explore choices and the learning process doesn't just begin, it continues to develop from where you are now. Often, we as adults find a handful of things we like and we quit exploring. We are treating ourselves as if we are exercising the freedom of choice while not entirely exploring the freedom of our choices. We sometimes don't see a need in ourselves to be adventurous anymore in certain areas of our lives. In the process, life becomes just everyday, ho-hum, less than what it could be, and often dangerously void of options.

Many have traded life as an adult, with its adult responsibilities, for lack of artful living.

It's worth asking, *why do I need to keep exploring?* In short, you don't. But again, I've met so many people, that upon finding out I am an artist, they open up in the kind of ways that tell me there are a lot of people out there in a state of creative starvation. Many have traded life as an adult, with its adult responsibilities, for lack of artful living, when they can have both and improve their happiness significantly. Their tanks are empty. Then they see art and they light up, wanting to be enriched. I talk to them and share that they can be creative if they wish to be and even if not, they can raise their creative appreciation and quality of life.

If you find yourself feeling empty, please ask yourself why? You can be emotionally, spiritually, and professionally empty, but trust me when I tell you, you can also be artfully or creatively empty as well. Sometimes it is on purpose, but more often we are just putting one foot in front of the other on autopilot. Life should never be that mundane. Tell life and the universe what you want. Maybe your dream was always to have and raise children, and now they are grown with lives of their own. Where does that leave you? Trust, plenty of people are asking themselves this, and plenty turn to creativity to energize their lives. It's powerful medicine with no side effects, other than learning something new and rewarding yourself in a new way.

CHAPTER 4

The Beauty Creativity Brings Us

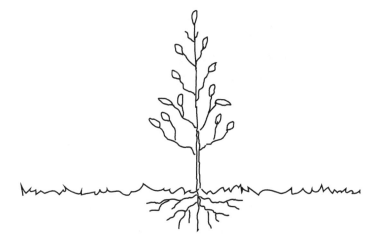

Stop and smell the roses.
Or even a flower from a weed.
The beauty that surrounds you,
Offers the vitality that you need!

BEAUTY CAN BE DEFINED as something which is aesthetically pleasing. But it is so much more complex because each of us individually defines what we see as beautiful in our own special way. We are deeply wired to put our own spin on the definition. Our own tastes too! Complexity aside, we all recognize things of beauty. We all see things we are attracted to, and that which is aesthetically pleasing may also be intellectually pleasing as well. Much of art is this way. We not only see its beauty, but we also recognize the skill in which it was created and the message it may be sharing.

One living thing inspiring another to create more beauty. Now there's a full circle, and one worth investing yourself in!

Possibly deeper ingrained in our being is that we see many signs of beauty in nature. We see the artist's talent, but we are met with a choice of this artistry being one of evolution or the hand of God. I will not delve into that thought deeply here, but there's little question the process of nature's beauty was filled with originality! To see the wings of a butterfly is amazing, and more importantly, butterfly wings have inspired countless pieces of art throughout the years. One living thing inspiring another to create more beauty. Now there's a full circle, and one worth investing yourself in!

In the fast-paced, technologically advanced, overly manufactured, throw-away world we live in these days, things made by hand are a refreshing break from reality. Overlooked by many, handmade items are cherished by those who appreciate a greater depth. Think of it as wanting to immerse yourself in a lake instead of skipping a rock across it. To hold something handmade is to be in touch with artists and artistry and therefore art offers a much more visceral connection to your possessions.

The process of manufacturing is economically driven. There is always a formula in saving time and effort to lower costs or increase profits. I'm the first to acknowledge that manufacturing is not a bad thing overall, and in fact, in many cases manufacturing makes exact copies with precision. This is ideal when you want a thousand washing machines, but far less desirable when you want one of something with originality and character. Working artists care about cost and profits to a reasonable degree too, but it certainly isn't their driving force. Utilizing their imagination and skill by making something one at a time while using their hands is. They are usually quite driven to do this, and passionately so.

As artists are not robots, the human soul comes through. The imperfections of an imperfect world sounds too cliché, as it's not imperfection which makes art stand out. It's partially the lack of jigs or processes that allow for easy duplication, but it is more primarily the human touch of a skilled brain at work. If a pottery artist makes two pots by hand which appear the same, at best they can only be similar. Each was touched by the hand and examined by the mind of its creator. I think there's a cool factor in that. Its beauty, form, and function have a story. A story of a person interested in taking a lifetime to learn a skill, conceptualize an idea and follow through in making art.

Creativity creates beauty and creativity itself is a beautiful thing.

Art or artisan works shine most, though, when done with a narrative—a story representative of our humanity, one where the viewer gives a thought or a reaction to its uniqueness. A personal connection is what makes art a healthy possession or pastime. It's also a very personal choice. The choice to make something, maybe even something to be passed on through the ages. Creativity creates beauty and creativity itself is a beautiful thing.

As we evolve in our now throw-away society, bringing these types of unique objects into your life is to have an artful life—to live an artful life. It matters not if they are made with your hands or those of someone else, just that they are appreciated and valued by you as an essential form of human expression.

CHAPTER 5

Your Creative Voice

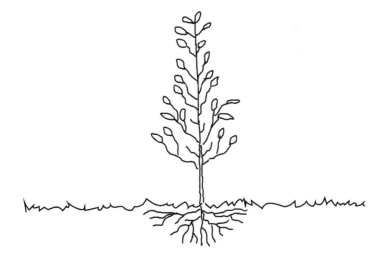

Speak in self expression.
Say it creatively.
We seek to understand you.
Verbal and visually.

NONE OF US CAN remember learning how to speak; how we pieced words together into a communicable language or how we pieced the words of others into something we could understand. This all took place before our recollections would allow. But as we did, our voices became more and more understood, as did the voices of others. No more crying to say we were unhappy for a range of reasons like being hungry or wanting attention, and no more laughter to broadly cover all of our happiness. We were developing a way to communicate our thoughts and emotions clearly and understand the cries and laughter of others with more in-depth detail.

I want you to think of art and creativity as a powerful super voice.

I want you to think of art and creativity as a powerful super voice. The concept of having a powerful new universal language at your disposal should excite you. Because, as with any language, your creative voice is a way to communicate your thoughts and emotions. But the best part about it is that it already lives within you. It really isn't foreign at all. Instead, it's untapped as of yet. Like any language, it too will take time to develop into a tool of communication. It is important to conceptualize, just as there is more than one language, there are many creative languages for your creative voice to speak in as well. Some speak with music, while others speak through paintings. Others still, even speak using the many languages the world already knows, verbally or through writing in a creative or narrative way. Often the words are so powerful, the world population demands that this powerful message is translated into many other languages. Yet, the pure essence of what is being communicated still lives within those words as a coherent message.

Possibly in a more traditional artistic sense, some also speak three-dimensionally, forming clay into objects to be seen from all sides, capable of showing surface contrasts and casting shadows. Some do so with a textureless surface, while others speak in high texture ones, with each thumb or finger's manipulation of the clay giving the completed work of art a different interpretation. These smooth or rugged surfaces or interpretations can not only bring a deeper depth of understanding about the subject matter itself, but the artist as well.

In other words, style becomes an artist's personal dialect, and just like other dialects, you can often see regional influences. Painters may do the same with the style of their brushwork or by choosing the effects of a palette knife across their canvas, cinematographers with mood and lighting, songwriters with lyrical phrasing and musical composition and rhythm, dancers through movement and actors through facial expression. These are all extensive examples of a way to speak, all meant to tell a story or create emotion, all a form of communication and all part of a creative voice everyone can tap into.

When you look at, hear, or read an artist's work, you can think of each of these disciplines in the same way as English, Spanish or French. Within each discipline, there can then be many styles of a similar subject matter, which in their own way can be thought of much like a different dialect of one particular language.

As an example, visualize three oil paintings of the same animal or scenic view, by three different artists. The results could be like hearing the same words spoken in English from the USA, the UK, and from Australia, because each artist has their own style, process and palette or colors. They apply the paint differently, using brushes and strokes of different size and shape, thus leaving a texture or being smooth as glass. They each have their own style and way of doing things, and it shows.

So while you can see each for what they are, each has its own, let's say, phonetic quality and may even require some patience in understanding their dialect or way of saying things. Make no mistake about it either, you very well may like one over the other. That is just being human. As with wine and even water, we all have our individual tastes, but this gives life flavor.

As with wine and even water, we all have our individual tastes, but this gives life flavor.

We all have the luxury of becoming artistically multi-lingual. It may not be easy, but we have the freedom to do so. We also have the freedom to have broad and diverse creative voices. In other words, the freedom to become artistically multilingual. We can communicate our ideas, thoughts, and emotions in many ways. We can be in a good or bad place and choose to express ourselves in positive or negative ways, just like any other form of language, and we can do so through all types of creativity. Ah, the true freedom of speech!

For those trying to find their creative voice, I say try different types of creativity. Try different things! But the number one thing I always say is, try separating the mechanical aspects from the imagination or idea part of it first. As an example, before you know how to move correctly when you dance, finding your coordination and learning steps can challenge your imagination to do so with the frustration of what I call the mechanics or the operational part of creativity.

Another example could be trying to paint and fighting the unfamiliarity of how the paint brushes are designed to work. This leaves many with a feeling that they are not creative at all and thus, it not only suffocates their creative voice, but it also kills it completely. What then follows are the wrong words: "I am not creative." Most of the time, this feeling is coming from not having the mechanical part (skill) mastered enough to form the words you want to say internally.

Think of it as the difference between learning how to speak and having something to say. I think everyone has something to say, but they may not have the patience it takes to learn a new language. Imagine it as if you were in a foreign country and unable to speak the language. You feel ignorant, because you do have ideas and thoughts, or places you want to go, but you can't communicate in an understandable way. This does not mean you do not have anything to say. It's possible you may even have very important things to say! So yes, creativity, artistry and living an artful life are the same as finding a new voice and learning a new language. Give it time though. The mechanical part does develop faster for some than others, but progress will come for all. Having confidence you have something to say is what counts the most. Be patient, but above all, remember to enjoy yourself. A creative voice is a great way to speak, and it's fun if you allow it to be.

> *A creative voice is a great way to speak,*
> *and it's fun if you let it be.*

For some, finding their creative voice may not manifest itself as actual creativity in the sense of painting or sculpting or alike. You might fall more toward the appreciative side of things, and yet, you really wish to be more artful. I say a fun way to begin is by turning to your own home and asking yourself if your home has a theme. If so, is that theme genuinely you or something from a magazine, or even from an interior designer you hired to represent you? When you or your guests enter your home, does the theme of your life come to mind or is your home simply the stuff of life? Think now—your theme might be family, it may speak of worldly travels, maybe it speaks thematically of where you live, as in a southern or southwest theme. So, does your home theme reflect the authentic you?

The word theme has real artistic meaning. Subject matter, ambiance, setting, idea, thoughts, even a recurring melody, all are descriptive words for themes. But they are all much further enhanced by a visualization. Creating a theme is simply best done visually, be it mentally or physically. Given this thought, think of those things in your home which prop up or support your theme and in doing so, support you. Your furniture, your color choices, even your house type. Ah, you might now be thinking style.

Style certainly can take on a theme, and a theme can certainly be presented with style, but for me, a theme is more to the point. You can have an African theme, done in a casual style. You could certainly have a southern living theme done in a high-society style. But no matter the style or the theme, nothing in your home, NOTHING, will make the point faster, more powerfully, or more personally than your choice of art, and guess what? It is usually the last thought of even the best interior designers who tend to work in style more than theme and function over artistry. A style is good, but a lifestyle is better! Especially one that reflects you!

Why? Why does function, as in a chair, sofa, table and so forth, within overall interior design, come before easily the most powerful driver of a theme? I wish I had the best answer, other than it's so personal a choice it is often simply avoided. It requires knowing the individual's taste. It requires a personal connection to emotion. It requires really knowing or caring to know someone and honestly, no one is better at that than you. Right? The choice needs your voice and don't think for a minute you wouldn't be better for voicing it. It again matters not if you paint the painting for the wall or buy the work of an artist, or even better, commission an artist to do something specifically for you. The crucial word in all of this is "you." It has to represent you and in doing so, your home will become a place that settles you down, brings you more joy and balance. I so completely believe this is a powerful and beneficial part of the *live an artful life* lifestyle.

Art, ladies and gentleman, has been coveted by modern civilization for centuries...

Art, ladies and gentleman, has been coveted by modern civilization for centuries. And a home without it looks empty of not only theme, but belief in a passion. Art gives everything else continuity. It not only stitches the fabric together, but it also puts the suit (or dress) right on your back. There's a good reason why every major city in the world is recognized for its art museums and collections.

I've kidded many times in a serious way by asking people, "When you visit a city as a tourist, do you visit the sofa museum?" Of course, their reaction is, "What sofa museum?" Exactly my point! But we have all visited art museums. Why? Well, using the sofa analogy, sofas, while capable of being attractive, function primarily for sitting, while the primary function of art is to be the cultural story of the human race.

While many things in nature can be beautiful, humans are the only living things creating art. It is one significant thing which separates us from other animals. Creating and or possessing art is solely a human thing. It is fair to mention that we are not the only living things using beauty or artfulness as a part of our society. Birds and butterflies, for example, use brilliant color and markings to attract mates, camouflage themselves, and more. Evolution has developed an incredible artful world in nature. But humans are the only animals who use nature as creative inspiration to decorate their homes, create art, take photographs, et cetera.

> *The primary function of art is to be the cultural story of the human race.*

So we see that nothing defines our home and who we are like the art we choose. Strong words? Yes, I suppose, but let's visualize some fun examples. Imagine a living room. It's beautifully furnished and seemingly complete in its southern living style. There, over the fireplace and beautiful wood mantle, is an enormous painting of an animated goldfish, amid a bright blue background. The frame is bright metal. Guests arrive, they enter the room, and what do you think is the first thing they will see? I'm sure you guessed the fish. And what might they be thinking? Okay, stay with me now. Same room, nothing has changed except the fish has been replaced with a big mirror.

So what do your guests see now? Well, if they see anything, it will be the ceiling. Mirrors are a noncreative or thematic choice, a throwback from days when nighttime interior light was poor, and a mirror's reflectiveness would double the candlelight and help people see better. They are not a piece of art.

So take the same room, here we go again. Replace the mirror with a glorious painting of a battleship or beautiful nude women.

I hope I have made my point that it does matter! And so, let's take our themed room and place a tranquil setting sun over mountains of deep blue, maybe a stately oak tree in a pasture of horses, a peaceful brook or a dirt road with a man or woman with their beloved dog taking an autumn walk. How about a beautiful garden filled with blooming azaleas and a sunlit path? When your guests come in that room, or better yet, when you enter that room from a busy day or hard day of work, which of my examples will feel most like home to you?

Visualize it and make it your theme. Find what grounds you and energizes you and your family. Find art that brings intimacy to intimate parts of your home. For me, a dining room is an intimate place. It's a place where you eat with family or friends, not strangers. The right piece of artwork can be wonderfully supportive of the table setting you choose and can bring people together.

It should bring you stress-free comfort, relaxation, solitude, peace, energy and refuel your soul.

Your home is actually a great place to unleash your creative voice too. If you create, your creativity is from within you, meaning something you enjoy. Above all then, your home should be a place to enjoy. It should bring you stress-free comfort, relaxation, solitude, peace, energy and refuel your soul. If you choose not to share your creativity with anyone, you should absolutely want to share it with yourself and your family, and your home is a ready, willing, and able place to begin. It's your blank canvas.

Last, if any of this brings out a notion of fear, crush it! There's nothing wrong with a little professional help with interior design, but the result should never be something that isn't you. Be verbal and use your creative voice to communicate your intended theme and lifestyle.

CHAPTER 6

Action, Process, and Fulfillment

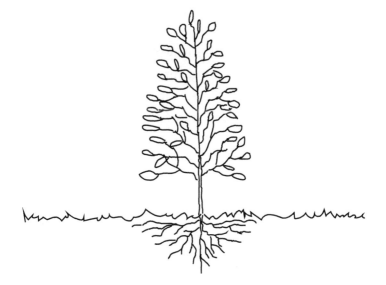

Lights, camera, action!
Your process tried and true.
Take charge with your achievements.
And with everything you do!

LIVE AN ARTFUL LIFE is itself a call to action. It's a jump out of the rut, overcome those obstacles, take charge and enjoy your life attitude. It's a commitment to avoid the mundane. For some, this may be a complete lifestyle change and perhaps to others, a much-needed lifestyle enhancement. Either way, I believe you owe this lifestyle to yourself, and if you are this far into this book, it would seem you do too! You deserve the happiness an artful life can bring you.

To *Live An Artful Life* is to grow and nothing about growth means standing still, even if your physical ability is hindered. Yes, you can grow without walking, because this action is as much about gaining mental traction as it is anything else. I've had the pleasure to meet several wheel-chair-bound individuals who are far from disabled. In fact, I've met many so-called mentally disabled people, who can be downright creatively inspiring!

The point is not to focus on what you do not have, but what you have and how you can creatively grow from there. This is important because you are searching for/or building your launching pad. Better yet, you need to plant your own seed to grow a new and improved you! One which not only goes up or climbs out of that rut, but one that blossoms profusely in a world of abundance! This is going to take good soil, plenty of sunshine and water. So get motivated!

You need nutrition.

The soil, in this case, would be your foundation. Let's face it, trying to grow in a mess of old dirt is hard. You need nutrition. Repotting yourself may mean cutting ties with things and habits that will hold you back, but hack away, you deserve a rich foundation. The reference to sunshine is all about inspiration, and that can be found almost anywhere, but you must be open-minded about wanting to be inspired. Just because the sun shines doesn't mean you will catch its rays. Don't just accept the light, seek it!

Some move through life only seeing a sidewalk, while others glance over and notice a garden. Still others visually scan, seeing every flower, butterfly, and bee. They find the secret garden! Observation is your friend here. Chin up, have a look around. Also, most people it seems find more reasons to complain than rejoice. Being inspired out of darkness is possible, but only if you want to create more darkness. Find a reason to rejoice, and the universe will have good reason to keep you on course.

You now have given yourself soil and sunshine, the last is water or your creative materials. Keeping materials at the ready allows you to flow through spontaneous creativity. You can instantly feed that hunger. A juggler needs things to juggle, right? Without, he or she is just a person moving their hands all about. Having materials at the ready allows you to act upon your ideas and more instantly find the gratification you seek and deserve.

With time, artists eventually find their creative process. One that comfortably suits their desire for creative expression. Whether you are just starting your creative life, or smack dab in the middle of it, it will become the way you go about doing what it is you do. Your process will be more than simple habits too. Rather, it's a reasonably stable foundation which you have developed and only time invested can make it yours.

Often I think this is one of those critical things new artists must navigate through as they find the right path for themselves. There's always the "What am I doing?" and certainly the "How do I do it?" But, those things are usually ever-changing, developing and growing. But things like how you warm yourself up, how you set up your studio or yourself, what materials feel best, your lighting, time of day, number of days in a row, quiet or music, to be inside or out, your references, your palette and so on, those things change very little, and everything else moves around this foundation. Again, though I reference painting a lot, a foundation is key to all types of creative expression and a creative lifestyle.

In my view, this doesn't matter if you are a painter, a sculptor, a potter, a dancer, a recording artist, an actor, or any other creative type. There needs to be a reliable process for which to create from, and the primary person putting trust in that process is you unless of course, you are a collaborator, then everyone needs to be on board.

In fact, the reason I think many bands break up is that deep within each principal member (John and Paul of the Beatles, Glen Frey and Don Henley of the Eagles) is their different personal processes to create from. When they blend, they make magic, and when they don't, they make trouble.

Go to your foundation first.

The same goes for you. If you find yourself unable to create or you're having problems with that which you create, or even more deeply, your life, go to your foundation first, not your subject matter or the how-to part of it. I'm not saying you'll always find the problem there, but it is imperative that you don't find the problem there before blaming other things. Think of it this way: you clean your studio and decide to move your easel to a new spot. A few weeks go by, and you are no longer thinking about having changed your foundation, you are wondering why you are out of sorts. Maybe as a musician, you changed the way you have warmed up for a gig, or perhaps the lighting has been changed in a group studio you share. Always go to your foundation first.

Now with this in mind, the other roadblock artists run into as we progress, become more confidence, and grow, is the tendency to take on more complexity. Again, it could be a faster rhythm in a song, more complex choreography, larger scale sculptures. Maybe it's much more complex subject matter. As this happens, it seems simple to say you should walk through projects in your head and visualize them first, but many people do not. They try and figure it all out as they go along and this can set them up for the painting-yourself-into-a-corner scenario. Listen, some good can come from mixing things up, but getting mixed up can also come from mixing things up. Be aware of your imbalance and how it may be working for or against you.

> *Be aware of your imbalance and how it may be working for or against you.*

In the end, creating art and living artfully can feel amazingly fulfilling. Even after three decades of creating paintings, I'm sometimes amazed that I was even the one who created some of them. Heck, I know Bob Dylan feels that way about some of his songs. Trust me, you really want to experience this feeling. It can be an out-of-body experience for sure. It's as if some parallel—you, or your internal twin—is there to surprise you. It keeps your ego in check too!

It's okay to feel special about your talent, but not so head- filled about yourself that you lose sight of the universe's role in bringing you ideas and life moments which allow your talent to really shine in its inspiration. To be artful is wonderful, to heal and grow from it is enriching, to share it is amazing, to be complimented for it is an honor, to make a living from it is a blessing, and to be surrounded by it is very, very special indeed. Creative fulfillment is a valuable currency which brings emotional wealth.

CHAPTER 7

Putting You In Your Artfulness - Emotion

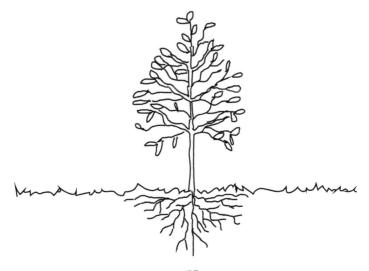

Your life is like your signature.
The autograph you make.
Express yourself emotionally,
Give more than you can take!

THE CREATION OF ARTWORK, in a sense, has no boundaries. It is so vast in its universe you really must make sure you have a true understanding of more than just technique, but yourself as well. For it is yourself you are expressing while venturing into any artistic medium. Every time you create something, it is the relationship with yourself in command of things. Losing sight of you in whatever you are creating removes the soul of your work.

Losing sight of you in whatever you are creating removes the soul of your work.

Proper technique on its own, while important, is nothing without what you bring to the table in the creative process. For instance, if four people paint the same subject matter or read the same lines of a script or move through the same choreographed dance, all being required to use the same techniques, or same materials, on the same day and with each other, you will still have four different results. Even if one is asked to paint or read or dance the subject first and the next artists are asked to copy the first's work and so on, each of the four outcomes will still be different. This is the wonderful human element we all bring to the creative process.

These differences could have something to do with years of experience. They could have to do with being left or right handed. They could even have to do with the artist's height and thus the slight difference in vantage point or length of reach. But it also has to do with things much more profound, like an artist's sensitivity to color, personal feelings, atmosphere, age, mindset, confidence, passion, needs, reasoning, relationships, experiences, beliefs and so on. These are all like power tools of creativity. Materials to create with and from are everywhere around us. It's what is within us that makes the world of art a reality.

The greatest technique in the world only allows for expanded ability. We all know there are many people in the world with ability who require minimal effort to get results. Others work very hard at it, while others never even tap into their talent or abilities in the first place. Even for those with born talent, proper technique is learned, but the understanding of you and wanting to express who you are must be felt. Some do as little as snap their fingers to a tune, some break into dance and some go as far as choreographing an amazing story. Different strokes for different folks, as they say. But's there's no doubting it—if you are trying to break through a plateau as an artist or artful person, have a look at yourself and really try putting you into your creativity. Don't just do, do you!

Don't just do, do you!

When a client purchases a painting of mine, I know without question they are not just buying a picture of a familiar place, they are purchasing my version of it. My personality is all wrapped up in that work of art, and my best advice is to make sure yours is too! If you take any type of creative class, you should first feel like you have something to say. Anyone can learn to paint with some reasonable level of success. It's feeling strongly that paint is the best way to express yourself, not just something to do. Then respect the teacher's technique, but understand you are not there to become a clone. You are there to become a better version of you creatively. That is the only way to truly grow as an artist.

What you bring to your artwork defines the narrative. Sometimes the story is more apparently realistic, such as a boy and his dog, or kids at the beach. But in less realistic artwork, such as contemporary genres, the narrative is even much more about the artist. Make no mistake, the narrative had better be there, for without it, you'll just have a lifeless rendering.

I always love when actors are being interviewed and the host asks them what they were trying to bring to their roll. No one simply says, "Me!" Think of the most iconic characters of stage and screen and ask yourself this; are the words "I'll be back" from the 1984 movie *The Terminator* iconic because of the words themselves, or because an Austrian bodybuilder-turned-actor spoke them in his thick native accent? Well, and then he backed up his words on screen, but you get my point. Songs get sung, and hits are made. Then others come along and cover the same song and another hit can be made. You make it your own. This is what makes your work relevant—worth creating, worth doing and then associating your name with it or even placing your signature on it.

Take a restaurant chain; walk into any of them and there is no surprise as to what you will find. It's a repetitive theme and they are all the same. Sometimes this familiarity has its merits, for instance if you are traveling and you don't wish to take chances. But take your favorite local restaurant and ask yourself why you like it. Even if both the chain and the local joint are just cooking burgers, it's more than just the food. There's a personality about the place that fits you. That's the importance of you in the equation. Your favorite place is as much about you as it is the place itself.

The Emotional Aspect

Artists have a way of playing off emotion. We get inspired by things that make us feel good or bad or provoke deep exploratory thought, and depending on our creative voice or creative expression, we deliver visual, audible, tactual and hopefully visceral works of art because of it. It is part what we do and what makes us tick.

A form or piece of art has many parts to it, but emotion is the key to it actually becoming art.

A form or piece of art has many parts to it, but emotion is the key to it actually becoming art. There must be more to it than simply placing paint perfectly, or a song sung in key, or just reading a script. The creation of art must come from within and extend through your hands, your voice, or through movement. It is the connection of your mind and soul that gives art it's power.

Some artists create from pure pain, trying to find answers to questions about the darkness in their life. Others create from the joy of life and their enthusiasm for it. While still others create from a deep emotional passion such as love, even an abstract love with texture, color or contrasts.

On a personal level, I think to myself that I have painted through amazing happiness, and yet, that happiness is but a layer in the many layers of the day to day, month to month, year to year bombardment of things hitting me. Some bouncing off, some penetrating.

I'm a pretty positive person, but my father passed away when I was just twenty-four. Has it ever shown in my art? Honestly, I don't know. Heck, my mother, a creative spirit in her own right, has been gone for more than eighteen years at the time of this writing. These things may result in an underlying pain or a great fullness and appreciation for life. I think my art reflects the latter of the two, but maybe one never quite knows.

I also think back on having painted through multiple recessions, wars, and natural disasters, along with the loss of good friends and wonderful pets. Does it show? Again, I don't have an answer, but my guess is it does. We are a product of our own lives and artists are capable of reaching deep. Those who appreciate art and the arts are undoubtedly drawn to more than just skill. They are usually also seeking something deep within themselves, as they experience an artist's expression.

On the other hand, my life has been filled with many blessings. The fact that choices throughout my life have allowed me a life of expressing myself is a wonderful gift, and I hope that every artist, or yes, even those who support the arts, feel this way.

Art, too, can be a powerful therapeutic tool. But I think one must be careful of how this tool is used. Self-therapy is very different than that which is done by a trained therapist. I'm by no means saying self-therapy is a bad thing. You just have to be mindful if you're making progress, healing and bringing yourself out of darkness, rather than digging yourself into a deeper hole. Art is often filled with solitude, and if you are trying to create your way out of a deep loss or sense of darkness and despair, a spiraling effect could trap you. It's likely best to collaborate with a fellow artist, a group or a guiding light.

In fact, often total immersion as in taking a workshop can be the absolute best things for the creative spirit! No matter your geographical location, there are excellent schools and even private workshops going on all the time. Would-be and seasoned artists sign themselves up to improve a skill, often benefitting from the camaraderie of a group's energy. Regarding emotion, hearing others' stories can make you feel validated, moving to a good vibe and rhythm, amazing joy, and fun. Lifelong friendships can quickly form in these environments and possibly also net you your greatest results. Sometimes rowing the boat along is what you need. Sometimes having a crew is powerful medicine.

If you sell your work, again, those who appreciate your work are seeing more than just skill. They may be seeing and feeling your story, or as most often is the case, I feel they are finding their personal connection to it. It is as if you have, without consideration, created a porthole or bridge for them to rediscover an emotional tie to their own life. I have watched many a person while looking at a piece of art for sale, not find an emotional connection to it and they just move along. That connection may only be in the form of pleasing color, but it's not just that you the artist is talented or skillful. There's more to it.

Emotion is a tool you can actually use.

Art is emotion. It is storytelling. If you are invigorated by your creativity, yell "Charge!" and have a great time! If, though, you are pondering, second-guessing, or just not feeling right about it, take time to look within yourself by looking directly at your art and your foundation. Have you become monochromatic? Are you starving or limiting yourself? Are you creating small instead of big or vice versa? Are your compositions repetitive? Is your contrast harsh, echoing a similar reality? Are you feeling or seeing stagnation? Is your art saying what you want it to? All art forms of art apply here. All can show your soul.

Annually, we wish for a New Year's resolution, when in reality each day is a time for evolution. Emotion is a tool you can actually use. Like any tool, it can be misused or overused, but used correctly it keeps life interesting and your creative self too! Look inward, but reach outward! Value the creative currency emotional wealth brings and remember the you in what you do makes your creativity special. Don't miss it—you're worth having around.

CHAPTER 8

Overcoming Obstacles

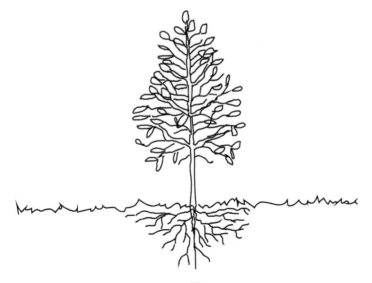

Don't let life hold you back.
Don't let it get in your way.
You got this, so go for it.
Hurtle it today!

WHEN I WAS A young boy around three or four, I owned a very special toy box. It would be fun to call it a magic box with a genie that appeared from within, but in truth it was only a shoe box filled with a bunch of Cracker Jack toys from the 1950s and 60s (back when there were really good toys inside), Matchbox cars and trucks, and other assorted odds and ends like Army soldiers and that sort of thing. They were just kid things, but collectivity, they were also a fast track to adventure!

The adult in us today doesn't really see the magic box anymore. The magic box we see as a child becomes invisible—hidden in a pile of responsibilities. But trust me when I say this; that box was truly more than small little toys in an old shoe box. It was the key to unlocking the door of a young boy's fascination with imagination. It was a whole world to enthusiastically venture into; a very close friend, and so much fun. For me, it was a Harry Potter book a half-century before its time. Magical? You bet it was!

Later in life, my mother would tell me stories about taking me places with her. She said, "Tommy, you were the best child. I could bring you places with your box, and you would sit down, remove the lid and be swept up into your own little world for hours." She would go on to say, "Those hours would pass without protest as you played, and when it was time to go, one by one each item would go back in the box, the top would go on and off we would go. You were a wonderful child." Thanks, Mom, and thank you, magical box! You see, the box was simply a tool for my active imagination.

As with most kids, I was the firecracker and toys were the lit fuse! That fuse could have been a coloring book with crayons, an old guitar, or a shiny bike. The same rings true as an adult, only it could be a car, your home, or your closet of clothes.

Some years ago, my wife Linda and I were waiting at the gate for a flight at Washington/Dulles airport. A small girl around the same age I was when I had my box, sat on the floor and played much the same as I once did. She didn't have a box of goodies, but she did have a playful imagination and with her small Snow White and the Seven Dwarfs toys, she ended up turning her shoes into a bed and even a boat at one point, sailing around the floor and having a big time of it.

Thirty minutes at least were preoccupied with her own imagination. No one else played any part in the development of the characters or their journey. It was both amazing and charming to watch, as her thirty minutes or so of amusement became mine as well. You could hear little sounds and songs softly come out of her mouth. On her own magical journey, carrying her places all of us should be so happy to go.

Children are carefree. If you look at the basic definition of the word carefree, it pretty much says it all; free from anxiety and responsibility.

Why is it children can do this and adults have a much harder time of it? Once again, the simple answer is *children are carefree*. If you look at the basic definition of the word carefree, it pretty much says it all; free from anxiety and responsibility. I like to think of being carefree as not being "controlled" by anxiety and responsibility. Frankly, this is a lot more about responsibility, which is where much of the actual anxiety and stress evolves for some.

At this point, I am not going to pretend to be a physiologist, but it is fair for me to speak from experience when I say; we all have big doses of life (ego, pride, dreams, family, jobs, etc.), which we allow to control our complete sense of creative freedom. Even career artists are affected. Millionaires are also not immune, so this is not all about money. It is about choice. Anyone of sound mind can visit their imagination and choose to be creative if they wish. It is free and yours to do with as you please. *Please note;* the word *please* can also be found in the word "pleasure."

So imagination comes with a lifetime of free admission. Not many really good things are free. Not many truly powerful things can be had for free either. Yet one of the most powerful, really, really good things, is 100% free—your imagination. It can take you places no jet can, calm or excite you like no medicine ever will, it has no unhealthy side effects, and it can teach you things no book ever will, especially about yourself. In use, it is the basis for real thought and certainly all ideas. It is uniquely yours as well. As mentioned previously, your imagination is 100% made of only those things you have put in your mind and the ideas generated by those thoughts. Knowledge and inspiration feed it. Wow, give me some of that, right?

That is the essence of imagination and ideas, blending things you know into a wonderful recipe, and it's the best reason to continually "feed your imagination."

You might imagine a building made of whipped cream and cake, but without having experienced those two things in some fashion, you simply could not imagine or fantasize about them. You only know what you know. Knowing about buildings, whipped cream, and cake gives you the tools to put them together, to imagine them as one if you wish. That is the essence of imagination and ideas—blending things you know into a wonderful recipe, and it's the best reason to continually "feed your imagination." Another reason to start feeding your imagination is it is the fuel that should be powering your creativity.

Now the difference between your imagination and creativity is this: while your imagination has no boundaries, your creativity may very well have a harder time of this. Thinking big is a lot less troublesome than creating big. Your imagination may see that building with so many stories, each made of whipped cream and cake, with an elevator that goes to the moon. Creating this building, however, is another thing. Knowing how to use the limits of your imagination and creativity at any one given time is a valuable way of enjoying and making use of both.

If your imagination only lets you be creative in a monumental way, you may think of yourself as a big thinker, but you would be missing the bigger point. Small things count too, and creativity need not always be a marathon. In fact, as an adult, it is that marathon attitude that stifles most creativity. A child might be happy with doodling a small and imperfect apple, where an adult often thinks they need to paint a whole bowl of fruit, perfectly, on their first try or deem themselves no good and uncreative! You heard me! You will also hear me say this; adults are often too results driven. Now add in life's adult responsibilities and well, many are finished before the race even begins.

The two biggest differences between children and adults are that adults are tasked with repopulation and serious responsibility. Some also might say maturity, but we all have seen some adults act like kids. The population responsibility aside, regular day-to- day responsibilities are enough. We are taught some responsibilities when we are young, but their meaning becomes survival as we become adults. Don't have a job, you become homeless. This fear often drives us from the ability to have pleasure and to be carefree.

This fear often drives us from the ability to have pleasure and to be carefree.

This all feeds on itself. Our parents expect us to perform; to do well in school. Our schools expect us to perform and move up grade through grade, to then become employed and a productive part of society. Our employer expects us to perform as well, and we, in turn, expect to be compensated for our time. Our government expects us to obey laws, be model citizens, and to pay their taxes. That's the stick getting bigger and bigger, and then there's the carrot part of it. Money, our reward, an "A" grade, a gold star and a pat on the head. Then there's a house, maybe children, and the responsibly grows. The plot thickens, as some will become no more than a mouse running on its wheel in the cage of life.

So, results-driven performance is ingrained in our being from an early age. We learn about wanting things and all forms of currency. Some kids even effectively learn that bad behavior can get you something you want faster than good behavior will. You cry, the sucker goes in your mouth, reinforcement begins. Results are results when you are young, but children are still much more love, fun, and experience-oriented than their adult counterparts. Carefree.

Don't get me wrong—kids like toys and things, but adults often need bigger and bigger things to fill the void of not being a kid again. The bicycle becomes the first car, and then there's an apartment which becomes a house. This all takes money, which begins the lifelong job search, and with new jobs comes more responsibilities AND desires. This becomes new furniture, vacations, status, titles, more money, more bills, kids, more bills and hey, now you're up to your ears in it until you retire and get off the merry-go-round. This is all results driven, and for some, it can be hard to shake. Being too results driven raises expectations and therefore may even have you chasing levels of perfection in search of elusive rewards.

It's easy to say here, so what's the harm in this? Well, adults learn what they know over an extended period of time, incrementally. It's called a career for a reason. What is forgotten when it comes to a hobby or expressing your untapped artfulness, is that we tend to seek instant gratification. So you might decide to take dance lessons. Up to this point (throughout the years), it's been going really well with this carrot and stick thing.

As such, you march right on into the class, being the seasoned, ladder-climbing professional that you are, and expect to swish your feet around all over the floor and *voila!* You expect to be a dancer! Sounds easy, right? Then reality sets in. One and two, one and two, one and two—*whose feet are these anyway?* Two and three and four—*I swear those look like my shoes down there, but, but…* one and two, three and four—*okay, now this is not funny, I'm not looking at all like the "Dance Like the Dreamer That You Are" videos I purchased. &%^%^$$!! It must be this instructor! I just don't understand. OH NO, I'm not a dancer!!! I knew it. I must not have any creativity in my whole body. Oh hell, I give up.*

Creativity shouldn't feel like work.
When it does, that should be your indicator that
you are trading the fun for frustration.

This is the point where I tell you in my humble opinion, that most of the hobbies we try and fail at as adults are because we are too results driven. Of course it's okay to want to be good or even master something, but creativity shouldn't feel like work. When it does, that should be your indicator that you are trading *the fun for frustration.*

Allow me to make this next example. Let's say you enjoyed reading and wanted to do more of it, so you joined a book club. But, being so results driven and thinking you had such a natural gift for your love of reading, you didn't seek just any book club, you chose one where everyone there only spoke Greek and read only read Greek titles. Okay, assuming Greek is not a language you speak or understand, it is still a language, and you do at least speak English. So, you venture into your first meeting with the club. Which do you suppose it will be—fun or frustration? Bingo! This has frustration written all over it.

So now, let's say you manage to make it through a few meetings, but the frustration level is too high, and you quit. A month or so passes, and someone asks you if you want to join their book club, and you say, "Nah, book clubs really aren't for me. I just don't do well in that environment."

Now, I have met many people that could take this example and mask it over the previously mentioned dance lesson or learning to paint, or learning guitar or anything you might seek for fun. They try to be artistic but quit after one class, deeming themselves completely uncreative. I also meet those who never even try, because one or both of their parents—or worse, a teacher—told them they were not creative or that they would starve if they took that path. I've met people who beat themselves up for this their whole lives, and I've certainly met people where this unhappiness even carries over into their work, which then actually keeps them from performing to their fullest there. For the record, this is certainly far from LIVING AN ARTFUL LIFE.

Change or growth happens slowly, but steady practice or doing pretty much anything over and over again does net real gains and measurable improvements in your ability.

You must always remember that as humans, we learn things incrementally. In fact, our whole society is built around incrementalism. Change or growth happens slowly, but steady practice or doing pretty much anything over and over again does net real gains and measurable improvements in your ability. This is why it is imperative to find fun in your ability at the time so that you keep going to the point of realization that you are indeed improving. Seeing, hearing, or feeling that improvement is the key to sticking with it.

Using our Greek book club example above, here are some interesting insights.

First, it's so easy to say if the choice had just been a club using the same language, all would have been a big success. Well maybe, and this certainly makes a point of not biting off more than you can chew. But even though my example was meant as just that, a radical example, there is something to be said for trying radical things. *Living an artful life* is not just about someone who likes painting or poetry. *Living an artful life* is about all of us experiencing life itself, especially in inspiring ways. Inspiring to not only yourself, but to others, and really enjoying life in the process.

Second, while you may not understand Greek, things are still being communicated. If you allow yourself to have fun and not be frustrated, your brain will try its best to learn, as that is what brains do. Remember, it's a book club, it's not your employment or a life-threatening situation. It is supposed to be fun. In the context of fun, at least you will have learned some Greek in the process, opening a new world and with time, found a new way to express yourself. But having fun is the key.

Let's use Spanish as another quick example. If you asked me whether I speak Spanish, in a literal sense, the answer would be no. But if we then went to a Mexican restaurant and when ordering I said; *dos tacos,* or *uno burrito por favor!* I would have at least been somewhat communicating in Spanish, right? I would be willing to bet, if you spent a year in Mexico having to eat the food and order in Spanish, you could pick up a fair amount of usable language. It's that total immersion thing. You become more fluent as you go along with anything, including your artfulness!

I also believe as radical as my Greek book club example was, if you kept going for a year, having fun without being results driven, but instead being *results rewarded* in happiness, I truly believe you would become pretty good not only with the Greek language, but the culture as well. One could say the same of dance, painting, or anything your artful life could offer.

Third, most things like this have the dual purpose of immersing oneself into a possible hobby, yet often just as important, in building relationships. I venture to say those book clubs are just as much about people and the relationships made, as they are about the books themselves. Best, of course, is to find harmony in both. But let's face it; the enjoyment of being with other like-minded people and sharing a passion for something can be a big part of the fun.

Still others wish to *live an artful life* in solitude, and there's just nothing wrong with this approach either. If you are enjoying yourself, again, that's your indicator. Most of my creative expression is done so in solitude. I'm by myself right now as I write, and it is a reasonable guess that a healthy amount of the art created around the world is done by one person acting alone on an idea they wish to express. The key to solitude is to make sure you are not there because you have to be. It must be a choice. You don't want to be alone and be lonely. If you feel lonely while creating alone, that instantly tells me you need to choose some form of collaboration where what you create is a team effort, like taking group studio classes.

Time alone, though, can be a personal growing experience and a healing one too, if needed. It's kind of interesting, but I figure all of the painting I do is a form of practice, even if it's a painting that is for sale or that has been commissioned. These days, I'm still in a form of creative maintenance, which is mostly what practice is for the experienced artist. I say *mostly* because my practice is also a time to be exploratory. A time to try hitting that high note without the audience. But I'm always exploring anyway. I love the added challenge, that little dose of risk.

The danger all of us have to avoid is becoming mechanical and losing the emotional side of creativity. You just do the same thing over and over and stop reinventing yourself. This can happen easily when you are working alone, but teams can have it happen too. It's the falling-into-a-rut syndrome. If I could say anything about someone who is off course in their *live an artful life* endeavor, it would be that of a person or persons, a family, a team or office group, who have found their way into a rut.

Imagine a pole in the ground. From it is a twenty-foot rope tied to your waist. You start walking, circling the pole for a few minutes. All of us have those times in our lives when we wander around a bit. Times when we render, rather than create. You keep walking around the pole, around and around and around. There's an old saying in the art world that goes like this: "If you render long enough, you will render yourself useless."

As you keep walking around the pole of daily life, there comes the point where your spirit is no longer intact.

Some even call it a comfort zone, but frankly, it's not really comfortable, as much as it is just life with the volume knob on low. The repetitiveness of a life's day to day can make your levels of satisfaction diminish. If you keep walking in this circle long enough, one day that rut is six feet deep, over your head and all you see is an earthen tunnel. You have, in essence, dug your own grave. The trouble for many is it's hard to know your new normal isn't normal at all.

To *live an artful life* is to cut that rope and no longer have your sense of direction guided by a tether. It's your chance for personal freedom. In the 1950s, kids who liked planes could buy an inexpensive balsa wood model plane. With quick assembly, he or she could throw it in the air, and it would whirl around for a matter of seconds before gliding to the ground.

Then someone creatively attached a plastic propeller to the front of it and stretched a rubber band the length of its fuselage. Taking your finger, you could wind the propeller until it was wound into knots, creating tension in the band for it to become a power source. Throwing it in the air, it would now fly propelled on its own for a minute or so as the rubber band unwound itself.

As time went on, little motors were created which would really propel the prop and the plane at higher speed, but there was no way to control it. So, the idea was to put the plane on a tether, and you were the pole in the middle with the plane circling you. Depending on how long or short your cord was to the plane, this could be a dizzying experience. Even though you could affect altitude, the attraction of speed and sound soon wore off and endlessly circling quickly found the rut of boredom.

Someone needed to cut this cord, which led to the invention of radio control. Then, flight really took off! Neither creativity, nor life, is about endless circling, or for that matter, seconds of simply gliding to the ground. All of these things are about having enough propulsion, control, and freedom to make your life an adventure. With that tether finally cut, the rut is gone. Now there is a limitless ability to soar and to explore creatively. Not only can there be proper takeoffs and landings, but loops, spins, stalls, and yes, crashes too. It's all part of life.

> *To live an artful life is to grow through experiencing the power of creativity, the freedom of imagination, and sharing your inspiration with others.*

To *live an artful life* is to grow through experiencing the power of creativity, the freedom of imagination, and sharing your inspiration with others. That is a good reason for being alive. Not to glide or to be tethered, but to fly. The key here again is to not fall into a rut, endlessly circling. If you eat the same things or same type of food over and over and over again, you may still like it, but will you love it? Will you ever know if you love something else more or even less for that matter? Validation through creatively experimenting can be the most freeing an experience you'll ever find.

Challenging yourself is the adventure of life. No, you do not have to jump out of a plane or climb to the highest summit, but knowing it's an option in itself is very empowering and a good thing. In artful life coaching, one of the things I most often find with people under stress is that they have lost sight of their options. They're not only in a rut, but they are also very unhappy there and have no idea how to find their way out. They see themselves in a profession, with bills to pay, kids, the dog, the beautiful home and unhappy or worse, wealthy and still unhappy. If you *live an artful life*, unhappiness is possible, but you possess the tools to fix what is broken. Your mind uses your imagination as a tool, your imagination uses its resources to become creative, and with creativity comes options and opportunity. The visionless become visionaries!

Now then, I must say, as primal a fear a human can experience, creativity for many seems to sometimes rank up there with public speaking. Yet I believe the difference is that most of us would actually love to be more creative while few have a desire for public speaking. Interesting enough though, I feel they are somewhat connected.

Years ago, I started using painting as a team-building exercise. I have stood with many very accomplished adults and experienced their apprehension as they simply hold a paintbrush, loaded with paint, in front of a fresh canvas. What is it that we fear as adults, that we did not as children? Paint brushes, for example, are not sharp or considered dangerous. Ahhh, but the results can be, and therein lies the problem.

Like public speaking, we feel we will be judged by our results, and this brings fear to an otherwise freeing activity. The years of watching adults hold that brush sort of became a personal experiment in understanding who and what we become as adults. Some, with huge personalities, would take the tiniest amount of paint and touch it to the canvas sparingly. While others, maybe small in stature, might wield the brush like a sword. But overall, there was just a great sense of not wanting to screw up!

So what is in us as adults that suppresses our inner child and our creative maturity? Well, I believe we become confident in our job, our title and position, but also invested. From the time we leave school and embark on a career, we gain confidence slowly through our experiences and accomplishments, which is all backed up by our title and compensation. In so many cases, what we do is who we are, or who we have become, and anything that may tamper with this is shaky ground, putting us on the verge of stage fright.

The reason many adults don't like public speaking is the same reason many don't like dancing. They don't want to look like an idiot, and I'm convinced that creativity instills a similar social and personal intimidation. Yet, somehow you may have noticed a little alcohol becomes like a magic elixir to our inner selves in these situations, and has us dancing about, but that is another story!

To be seen as creative is to be seen internally through external expression.

That connection mentioned above, between public speaking and creativity, is not only fear of reputation or looking like an idiot in one's own mind. I believe an even deeper connection is rejection. What makes an artist truly an artist is their ability to put themselves out there. To be seen as creative is to be seen internally through external expression. One isn't creative from the outside inward. One becomes creative from the inside out. Creativity is all about taking our internal selves, our thoughts, our inspirations, our experiences, and making something which lives outside ourselves—be it art, a book, a dramatic act, or a dance or a song.

Out in a world where it can not only be seen and certainly judged, but also provoke the thoughts, attitudes, and opinions of others, or even inspire the masses. We know as artists that this can carry a penalty in those reactions and rejections. We also know we can't stop any of it and it also can bring very positive reactions and personal growth.

In a world where the talking heads deliver mostly devastating news of humanity in 24/7 fashion, through the wall-mounted televisions that often are placed where art used to be, artists offer the age-old alternative of self-expression, a freedom everyone still possesses, in this country anyway. In service since the 1950s, television and our fascination with screens of all sizes is without question a very powerful form of communication. Creativity and art though, have been doing a pretty good job of it for the last several thousand years. And frankly, art always be a better way of communicating with yourself.

Care not about rejection. Hurtle your way over it and have a little fun in the process.

So let the fearful become fun-ful. Instead of screen gazing, get a brush or a piece of clay and make a mess. At least it will be your mess, and I promise, you'll be better for it. Care not about rejection. Hurtle your way over it and have a little fun in the process. By the way—you can also write, act, dance, sculpt, arrange flowers, sing, become musical, take photographs and so, so much more! Parents, you have the added luxury of having your kids show you the way!

CHAPTER 9

Being Resourceful, Problem Solving, Visual Awareness

Be resourceful
And visually aware.
Problem solving is knowing
Options are always there!

MY WIFE LINDA IS always saying that I'm resourceful. Well, I think she is too, and we play off each other's strengths that way. But what's really behind this resourcefulness is my creativity and experiences. Creativity is largely about being resourceful, and resourcefulness is basically creative problem-solving. I think visual awareness is key.

Being visually minded helps you see much quicker through an unsolved problem to a resolution or a way to achieve a goal.

Being visually minded helps you see much quicker through an unsolved problem to a resolution or a way to achieve a goal. Additionally, it's seeing what you have on hand and in the way of options which may help you accomplish a task. I'm not saying these are the only attributes needed in problem solving, but very important ones nonetheless. It's a bit like being in a maze, but at the same time visualizing it and it's possible pattern from above. This tends to help you more broadly consider your options, not just a narrow focus of possibilities. It's a clearer path to a solution. Visualization can benefit everyone, and it can be learned.

Try standing in your bedroom, closing your eyes and imagining your path to outside. One clear path will come very quickly. It's likely the way you always go. It may or may not be the shortest, but is now a habit. Now let's add in some panic. As you stand there visualizing, what if I told you there was a dangerous obstruction to your normal path? Could you visualize a new path? More importantly, could you do it quickly? If you can clearly and quickly see a new path in your mind, you are resourceful. If the new path even required stacking and standing on pieces of furniture, or other objects to get out, you are even more resourceful in your utilization of tools and implements for success.

Sometimes you can see professional athletes mentally and physically visualizing what they are about to attempt. Their head and hands may be recreating what they are about to attempt, such as a gymnast for a floor routine or a golfer on a green, getting down and lining up a putt. Artists need to line up the putt as well. I will share that 40% of what I create as a painter is done by way of commission. This means the subject matter is someone else's vision and I am the facilitator. I'm not painting what I want (in a sense), I'm painting what they wish to see, but cannot do themselves.

So the subject matter I receive is ever-changing, and there may even be complex new things to learn and so, I never just take a shot at it. I visualize it first, I line up my putt, and frankly, I paint at least 70% of the painting inside

my head, over and over before the part that really counts—
doing the real painting!

Now you may be asking, "Why only 70% in his head?"
Well, it's like this: First, you don't want to simply render a
painting (or your life for that matter). You want to create it,
and if you know every detail, rendering is all that would be
left. Second, creating should still be an organic process. As
an example; you can rehearse a play, but you know it will be
different in front of an audience with their surprise, laughter,
or emotional delivery. You want at least some of that emotional
anticipation or surprise as an artist. Third, you also want
discovery. Basically, you want to know your way, but you also
want to find your way, and you know what? With all that I have
shared here, you'll always have times where the final creation
is different than you visualized and that's okay, because that's
what art and an artful life is all about. But it shouldn't necessarily feel uncomfortable, it should feel exciting.

Your process and visualizing help stabilize it all as your
work of art becomes a reality. It's basically a kind of risk
management program. It's balancing the skill you have with
your desired results, and the spontaneity needed to keep
things alive with energy.

Dancers practice choreography over and over until
their routine is natural and their movements are fluid, and
they are not lost. But trust me, they feed off the energy of
the room to truly bring it to life. Here's a jazz analogy: if
you know your instrument, when your time of improvi-
sation comes, you find your way fluidly. You don't know
exactly where you are going but you feel your way through

it effortlessly. Everyone, in general, should visualize, and it's an important part of being resourceful.

Your process and visualizing help stabilize it all as your work of art becomes a reality.

With resourcefulness comes a general understanding of how a lot of things work. Creative people often have to figure out how things work by experimentation and even learning by failure. This trial and error mentality builds good references to rely on when problems arise. Where art is concerned, many fear a mistake while learning because they don't want to screw up the very thing they should be learning from. Mistakes are valuable lessons. We all make a series of them regularly. Sometimes it's a wrong turn, leaving our car keys as we walk out the door, or having something slip from our hands. Mistakes make you aware of your vulnerabilities, but if properly stored in our mind, we repetitiously avoid them and hopefully make wiser decisions. We learn from our mistakes.

Mistakes can also bring exciting bouts of serendipity. Forgetting something, and when going back, we meet an old friend, catch an important call, avoid a danger we might have otherwise encountered. With art, we may discover a new color or technique, create a masterpiece, and yes, find a solution to a problem we've been trying to solve. So, mistakes can also be wonderfully beneficial to resourcefulness.

Practicing resourcefulness is like practicing anything else. The repetitious action of doing anything cements the how to's in your life so that when the time comes, visual awareness offers you your options! Now, you may see some of those options riddled with compromise. If you had to jump from a second-story window each day to leave your home, that would not be a good compromise. But if your house were on fire, that would be a very advantageous compromise, and I'd say a very good option.

Advantageous compromise is part of problem solving too. Again, like creativity and visualization, it is not all, but part of the formula. It's about the basic trade-offs of moving forward versus standing still. As with the carrot-and-the-stick scenario, where the carrot is a solution and the stick is the perplexing stress and outcome of doing nothing.

I suppose for some unwilling to move, that stick may hurt less than actually making a decision. I suppose for them that pain then is all right to endure, as long as others aren't bothered or hurt by it. Still, this gets back to advantageous compromise, because any prolonged decision is a compromise of one's self or issues. Most important is that compromise should not happen simply out of exhaustion. It should arise out of the open-mindedness in finding a solution and achieving results.

Resourcefulness is much better found looking in the direction you want to go, and I think life is much more fun that way.

An ore can be heavy, but its weight much less so within the achievement of rhythmically moving a boat. Place a hungry shark behind your little boat, and you have "the stick" and place a beautiful beach with palms and a Tiki bar in your sights, and you have "your carrot." Resourcefulness is much better found looking in the direction you want to go, and I think life is much more fun that way. It sure always makes that ore feel lighter. Just as much fun is achieving results as a team and realizing that we all have resourceful strengths. Teamwork is all about trusting the skills, capabilities, and resourcefulness of others. Leadership is the asset management of those valuable characteristics.

So, there are many ways to practice resourcefulness and visualization. If it's a problem, creative or otherwise, try writing every option you can possibly think of down on paper. Often just seeing options can lend clarity to the decision-making process. It's much like the old artist's trick of doing many small compositional sketches to help you see one as a clear favorite, thereby giving you confirmation that it's the best decision.

As important is an honest desire to want the problem to be solved in the first place. As an example, if you need to lose weight, but you love eating pizza, you know you have a few options. One is to do nothing, as many do. You also have the option to stop eating pizza, to eat less pizza, to find some low-calorie pizza recipes, or to exercise a lot more. But you have to want to lose the weight, or a pattern of self-sabotage will keep you from achieving this or even making it a goal in the first place.

Make no mistake that resourcefulness and visual problem solving have broad life applications, not simply artistic ones. But those who live an artful life will mindfully adopt their benefits more often.

CHAPTER 10

Learn and Practice by Doodling

Doodle by day,
Doddle by night.
Doodling is fun,
And there's no wrong or right!

WE ARE ALL BUSY. If you have kids, or even aging parents who are absorbing a lot of your time, practicing or even getting started with creating any kind of art can be a bit of a challenge. For now, you need a way to feel creative though. Something that is not only impulsive, but easy to do. I think I have just the right thing.

Doodling, or random sketching, is one of the easiest ways to be creative.

As an artist, I talk to people interested in trying art all the time, and I tell them all the same thing I'm about to share with you. Begin by doodling. That's right, doodling! Stay with me now. First, doodling, or random sketching, is one of the easiest ways to be creative. It requires very little of anything. Very little time, no real talent, just a piece of paper, anything to write with, and of course, you! Doodling is helpful to anyone who does it, because the act of doodling is basically just getting random thoughts and ideas out of your head. Often they are unconscious thoughts. It is not as serious as true sketching; there are no doodling police to arrest you and no critics to tell you your stick figure riding a pony won't pass anatomy class. This even makes doodling perfect for those with disabilities or special needs, because they get to enjoy themselves without overthinking it all or having too many cumbersome materials.

Doodling has also been scientifically proven to be beneficial to thinking and widening our attention spans, with doodling control groups listing to information remembering about 30% more than their non-doodling counterparts. There's plenty to read on doodling, but my greatest piece of advice on how to begin is to not think about it. You can pretty much do it anywhere, just drop your hand on the paper and let it go.

I tell people to even turn on the TV and not really concentrate on your doodling at all. Just let your subconscious do its thing. I really mean that. Just let things come out of you, no matter the shape or subject matter—just have at it. I can share for instance that I have only been on a sailboat a handful of times in my life, but if you see me doodle, you will likely see a sailboat appear.

But doodling can be anything; any shape or line. There's no set amount of time to do it, just the carefree action of drawing. Make circles, squares, and triangles. Maybe stick figures or anything you love. Most of all, do not be critical of your results, as you will be completely missing the point of doodling in the first place. Doodling is meant to be a spontaneous and fun exercise.

You see, creating something big is exactly like running a marathon. It takes exercise, training, and lots of short runs even to start the marathon, much less finish it. But most of all, it takes dedication, and often dedication is not only about passion, it's about having fun. Heck, even the word *doodling* is fun, and if doodling seems like work, trust me, creating that masterpiece will be hell. But if it *is* fun, you'll want to do it again and thus, dedicate more and more time to taking the next step of really sketching something more accurately and growing as an artist. The better you get, the more serious your practicing will have to become.

Just because tools didn't exist at the time, doesn't mean those we call masters wouldn't have owned and used them.

Now, if you think this story is all about simple doodling, boy are you in for some more potential fun. For better or for worse, we are living in a digital world with new tools for creativity literally at our fingertips. Most of you still reading this story are probably crunched for time. I know this because the whole population seems to be feeling this second-by-second starvation.

So you're asking; even if I find the time to doodle, when will I find the time to expand on it? Well, my friends, time is about priorities and time management, and many of you already own a very powerful creative tool to help with this. The rest may want to consider it as I move along. It's called the iPad. What? You've heard of it? Just kidding, but of course, there are other tablets as well. The artist in me may be hearing the sound of simultaneous cheers and cries! Some saying, "I love my iPad," and others firing off purity projectiles saying, "down with digital!"

If you're a purist, I will only say this; I'll bet if Monet were alive today, he would very likely own an iPad. I'm speculating of course, but it's well known that Monet broke from tradition and was criticized for it. Just because tools didn't exist at the time, doesn't mean those we call masters wouldn't have owned and used them.

The iPad is not a traditional tool for creativity, but it is a powerful creative tool nonetheless. A big problem the creatively stifled have is time. It's not just time to create. It's time to buy materials, time to even find out what materials to start with or which medium to express yourself with. So the sprint becomes a marathon, and many are defeated before they begin, and so they never start.

But what if there was an app that would at least let you doodle, then sketch, or begin to understand color theory, even paint with an endless supply of materials? Wouldn't you be more likely to try? I think so, and it should not be considered a replacement or competing with standard mediums and forms of art, but instead another form and tool altogether. As an artist, I say, "Make the creative tools work for you, not the other way around."

As an artist, I say, "Make the creative tools work for you, not the other way around."

There are simple apps that are great for beginners, like ArtStudio, which allows you not only to get started, but to grow. As you do, you can try others like Sketchbook or move all the way up to amazingly complex programs like Procreate. The best news is the cost. In my opinion, an app like Procreate as a software program would be a deal at $250, but it's like ten bucks! If you own an iPad, you can afford a creative app, and from this simple step, help develop your artistry. It allows the beginner and most certainly even pros, to be spontaneous and develop ideas anywhere. To move quickly from one medium to the next, and once you've started, this will allow you to more easily move in a more creative direction by seeking classes and more traditional materials. Lastly, move past using your finger as a drawing tool quickly and purchase a stylus like the Pogo SketchPro, and you'll be on your way!

- **ArtStudio** - http://www.luckyclan.com/apps/artstudio-ipad

- **Sketchbook** - https://sketchbook.com

- **Procreate** - https://procreate.art

- **Pogo Sketch Pro** - https://tenonedesign.com/sketchpro.php

CHAPTER 11

Artistic Productivity

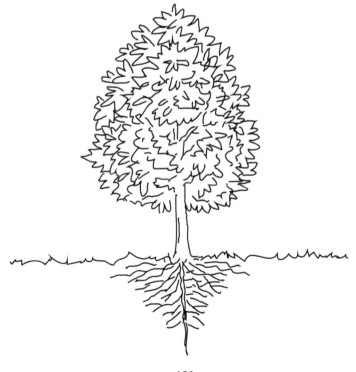

Being productive
Gets things done.
Adds to your practice
And is part of the fun!

TO ME, CREATIVITY IS an absolute blessing, but productivity may be my angel. As I have been highly creative all of my life, thankfully, I've been productive too, and as an artist, I want to share my philosophy in understanding the roles of both.

One question I've been continually asked as an artist is, "When do you work?" I think it is an interesting question because it feels like the type of question only an artist would be asked. I mean, you wouldn't ask those in most positions when they work would you? But I always have the same answer, and it's often met with some amazement. I tell them, "Monday through Friday unless I have to cut the grass midweek and then I might paint on the weekends a bit too." After all, I'm self-employed and can easily do so.

The point being, I treat my career as an artist seriously. I schedule myself as I think any employed person should and would. I may go on to say, "On occasion, I've started painting as early as 4 AM and I've painted as late as 10 PM," but it doesn't have anything to do with mystical creative urges that only come during a full moon. I'm just being productive.

Productivity is not some ugly side of creativity.

With that, many will say, "You actually seem to work a regular work week." Well, imagine that? You see, no matter what I've done, I've always intended myself to be successful and busy doing what I love. Productivity is not some ugly side of creativity, but let's also make no mistake about what productivity means. For me, it means diligently working at my craft and for my customers. It doesn't mean waiting for that mystical, magical creative bug to bite and it certainly doesn't mean banging out paintings. I never bang out paintings. I collect my ideas, funnel them down to paintings whose time it is to come alive and then paint them one at a time. I place everything I have in my soul as an artist into that one work of art through to its completion, and I am pretty methodical about it.

Do I give myself time to breathe? Yes, even during the painting process. I also give myself time to focus on other forms of creativity and my business and goals. But there's no mistaking it—this all is time management, more than creative management. It's all I can do to faucet my creativity; I have plenty of that. But we are all limited on time. Time management is an important life skill and an imperative one for efficient productivity.

I'm over three decades into the sales of my paintings. I was thirty-three when I started selling my paintings, though I had sold many other creative things I'd done. With a lifetime of creativity and business behind me, and a desired career as an artist and writer in front, I knew just being creative wasn't enough. Being creatively productive was a must. Everyone that works has to balance life and all that comes with it. Artists, especially ones with a desire for success, are no different. If you want to be successful at anything, you must apply yourself. It is work, but "if" that which you apply yourself to is what you love, it will not feel like work. This mindset to me is paramount to a good life in general. Don't be all willy-nilly about life; take the path of design and build the life you want.

> *Don't be all willy-nilly about life; take the path of design and build the life you want.*

There are many creative people in the world, but there are also creative impostors who may call themselves artists without actually producing anything but chatter. On occasion, a gallery visitor will come in with a friend, going from one artisan piece to another while saying, "I could do this, I could make that." Upon witnessing this, my wife Linda would (lovingly) say to them, "But you never will." She knows productive people don't talk about it, they do it.

She did this in support of the many artists she represented who productively used their creativity. Those who passionately enjoy seeing their vision come to life and also enjoy it becoming part of someone else's. In fact, many true artists have a hard time even calling themselves artists. They don't just toss the term around lightly. They know the title in its purest sense is earned, though they've already earned it.

I want to be open and clear with what I'm about to say. If you are creatively inspired, then create. If you are not motivated to create, you are not really creative because to be an artist, you must create. It is a call to action, a call to make something, rather than just thinking about it.

Is there such a thing as creative thought? Yes, but it's my feeling that many like to say they are creative thinkers. I say just thinking does not make you creative. Creative thoughts becoming things are what creativity is all about, be it art, a script, a song, a dance move, a software program, a garden, a beautiful room, a recipe, a new app, whatever! Your creative thought has to be part of the creative process to be valid, even if you are not the skilled part of the process itself.

If you design a garden in your head and others dig the holes and plant the plants, that was a creative effort. One couldn't happen without the other and you are therefore creative. But if a person comes up with ideas in their head and those ideas never see the light of day, calling themselves a creative thinker is improper in my opinion. Creativity cannot merely end with a thought; it is the act of doing something with that thought, idea, or concept that validates it as creativity.

If you come up with a fresh way to change up your family room and you get your kids to move the furniture, you are creative! But a person who comes up with the idea and it never happens is no different than the person that frustrated my wife by walking around pointing at artist's work and telling their friend they could do that. I say prove it! Be creative!

Okay, so let's look at the other end of things. Let's say you are not only creatively productive, let's say you also see it as a possible way to make a living. This means you want your creativity to become a business, one where you make a product in exchange for money or revenue. Then, by all means, manage it as you would any other business. All companies have to be creative, but they need to be productive too, and efficient in doing so. Successful artists just make creativity their business and treat it as such. You must apply yourself to become a better artist, and you must take time to learn business and productivity. You'll be happy you did.

CHAPTER 12

Your Perception of Success

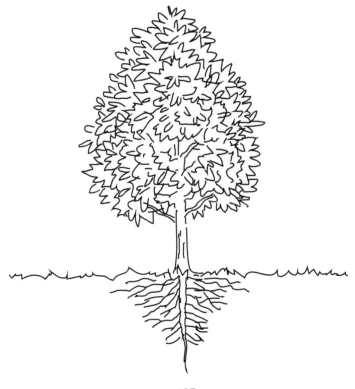

Know what success
Means to you,
So when you achieve it,
You'll know next what to do!

HOW DO YOU MEASURE success? Well, it frankly doesn't matter if you are an artist or not, but do you have a personal goal to measure your idea of success? Is it an amount of money, an achievement or skill, or maybe an award of some kind? The point is, have you given yourself the tools to even recognize your success when it arrives? If you haven't, will your success actually arrive at all? When you put your mind to doing something, you usually know when you've accomplished that task, right? But achieving success, or your perception of it, may be much harder to pinpoint, especially if you don't recognize it when it arrives.

Have you given yourself the tools to even recognize your success when it arrives?

You may find this interesting: I recently asked a few different friends, when they knew they were successful? They are all successful by its definition. All came from very modest backgrounds and became self-made millionaires. Their answers may surprise you, but teach us all something about success.

One said he finally was able to sleep comfortably through the night a dozen years after starting his company and certainly years after having significant wealth. He finally felt his company had a good enough financial cushion to make payroll and other expenses through the annual slow time his company would experience. Think about this now. His definition of success wasn't built directly on personal wealth, owning things, company market share, or business accomplishments. His success advice? *Sleep soundly.*

Another friend told me two really great things for his personal feeling of success. The first was humorous, but there's always truth in humor. He said when he had been married more than ten years and still lived with his wife. But then he also noted that it was when he was able to donate a lot of money to charity. His success advice? *Love and kindness.*

Now the other friend is the one I've already mentioned. While he spends a good amount of his time today working as a musician, he could have comfortably retired at thirty-five. The interesting part is he now admits all these years later, that he never really felt successful, rather, that he was always chasing success. That is to say, even though by all accounts he was very successful, he never honestly felt that way. Only now, retired and enjoying life, does he feel successful. He interestingly sighted that living below his means feels more successful than continually trying to keep up with gaining more wealth. His success advice? *Enjoy life, and live within your means.*

So, it would seem that being successful can be just as much work, or stress, as trying to become successful, and possibly even more so. Especially if you don't recognize that this is the case. The thing we all should value most today is a thing we are all born with: a limited amount of time. Success can be great, but it's only great if you recognize and appreciate it.

My wife and I have always self-prescribed ourselves to the five-year plan which allows for periods of satisfaction, reflection, recalibration, and achieving a level of success again and again—and realizing it. No one at thirty years old will know how they will feel about being forty until they are forty. You can guess how you think you will feel, but until you get there, you won't know. I think life seems more relevant and frankly more pleasurable, if you live it as you go without overthinking the future. No one really wants to be in a squirrel cage, but we are plenty capable at putting ourselves there, apparently even after becoming, by all rights, successful. A big part of success is just realizing you have options and choices along the way.

I think life seems more relevant, and frankly, more pleasurable, if you live it as you go without overthinking the future.

If your goal as an artist is to acquire awards and in doing so, you do not achieve a satisfactory level of financial success, have you achieved the success you were looking for? Well yes, awards were your goal. Because you may have failed at something else, doesn't mean you have not achieved your intended success. But it does validate our need to broadly understand success as an essential life tool. You can also experience selective success and not even know or care about it if the rest of your life is a mess. Or you can also be diligently working on a goal and successfully making significant gains, but not see it through a cloud of life's other responsibilities.

Linda and I are currently planning the next five years of our ever-maturing lives. It's a juggling act and an adventure at the same time. She has decided this is a good time to take up learning something new. In her case the ukulele. It's a fun little instrument, which on the face of things makes it quite approachable. But like any instrument, there's more to learn than meets the eye (or in this case, the ear). It is, therefore, easy to become frustrated, yet the good news is her openly saying, "I feel I am getting better." Success doesn't have to be the birth of an instant virtuoso. Finding enjoyment in learning and making incremental gains is essential. In short, having fun! Being carefree!

We were all born with a built-in and extremely important success gauge. Unfortunately, we all ignore it at some point or another, and some never look at the gauge at all again. It is, of course, the happiness gauge. No tool is better at letting us know how successful we are in our own mind and that's the only mind that really matters.

Perception is everything here. There will always be someone with more money and more things. Well, I guess this rule applies to all but about ten people on the planet, and if they are reading this book, I hope it helps them too!

But chase it if you want it. Just know when you have acquired it, no matter how large or small it is to anyone else. Realize it and allow yourself to feel successful in doing so, instead of replacing it with an empty feeling. That's the squirrel cage effect. Success should feel great, and the most important thing is not to let others define your success.

Feeling successful in the abundance of new ideas, creativity, and community outreach is a valuable currency in my opinion.

Feeling successful in the abundance of new ideas, creativity, and community outreach is a valuable currency in my opinion. Give yourself clear goals to achieve and make sure that you feel success in reaching those goals. Keep learning, ascend step by step, and reflect when you come to a landing. After all, stair landings (or plateaus) give you a chance to catch your breath, look back on your accomplishments, change direction, and ascend once more. Enjoy and *Live An Artful Life!*

CHAPTER 13

Improvement and Creative Longevity

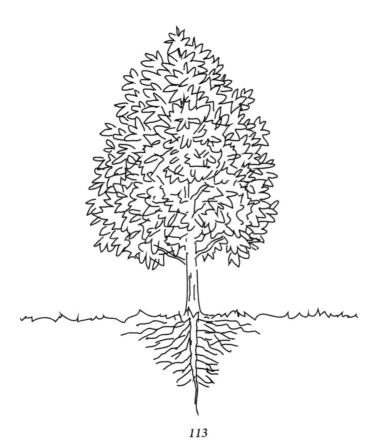

Home improvements
To the house of you.
Furnish brilliance
In all you do!

IMPROVEMENT. THIS ONE WORD is so true of creative longevity. Honestly, it may be the key to longevity, period. You know yourself pretty well. Now imagine a better you. Not a new you, but an improved you. Who wouldn't want a better version of themselves? A software update to version *YOU.2*, with new or improved features and security update! Count me in, right?

Who wouldn't want a better version of themselves?

Well, self-improvement is just that; a software update for your current operating system. And in the case I'm speaking about, a creative upgrade. One which keeps your mental dexterity and cognitive performance up to speed. The problem is, while most of us improve throughout life, we don't focus on our improvement as much now as working adults. We tend to focus on job titles and possessions, rather than skills and experiences. Artists, by the way, sometimes are no different.

Improvement in your artistic skill only comes in three ways: practice, expanding past fears or a comfort zone, or changing the way you express yourself entirely, such as switching from one form of art to another. With adult beginners who have forgotten their inner child, just getting started can be overwhelming. *What do I buy, which way do I turn, will I be any good?*

Then there's that person in your life who may have always mentally held you back with crippling comments like, you can't draw, you can't sing, you can't dance. It happens a lot, and it sticks to us way more than most of us think. So let me start by saying, brush that crap off and move on. They had or have no right to tell you that, and you are in control of you now.

> *Being artistic in any way is a skill—*
> *one that people can learn.*

Being artistic in any way is a skill—one that people can learn. Sure, there are some that will come into it easier, but this is the case with anything we learn. It doesn't matter if it's math or art. But with any skill, we have to just do it, and keep on doing it. You begin by just having fun, no pressure, let it happen naturally. You then enjoy yourself and understand you are beginning—you are learning a new skill. As you begin, especially with adults, it's natural to see you aren't a master, but don't be overly critical or hard on yourself. Let it be fun. When you are having fun, you want more fun. And in the case of learning a new skill, the more fun you're having, the better you get.

One day what was hard or frustrating is neither—you will have improved. You will be a better you than you were before you began. Depending on your age, you may have been doing what you do for a living for decades, and thus, you've forgotten the little improvements you've made in the professional you over the years. You start to think you are simply good at what you do. But it's mostly the case of doing it day in and day out for a long time. The skill in creating anything is the same. You improve as you practice, and sure, there will be hills and plateaus. But you'll get there.

I have actually already given you this whole next paragraph earlier, but I want you to reread it because you have already progressed by reading this book to this point. Here goes:

> You must always remember that as humans, we learn things incrementally. In fact, our whole society is built around incrementalism. Change or growth happens slowly, but steady practice or doing pretty much anything over and over again, does net real gains, and measurable improvements in your ability. This is why it is imperative to find fun in your ability at the time, so that you keep going to the point of realization that you are indeed are improving. Seeing, hearing or feeling that improvement is the key to sticking with it.

Drawing, painting, pottery, sculpting, singing, playing an instrument, acting, dancing, all take a fair amount of practice or hours to improve, but the improvement doesn't just come all at once after weeks or months; it happens gradually. Just like being around a puppy growing, you may not readily see the growth, but others who haven't seen the puppy so frequently see the change more easily. Often to see our improvement, we have to keep examples of the old us to compare with the results from the new us. Sometimes the improvements will be small and other times we will feel measurable gains. It's like ascending a flight of stairs, where the landings set us up to rise again, but if you keep going, rise you will.

Then we have those with years of artistry under their belts, seemingly not in need of much improvement. I would respectfully disagree, as we all should care to improve and grow. I think the happiest artists continually seek new ground, reinvention, rejuvenation, growth, and to broaden their scope and take on new challenges. Improvement is honestly part of artistry. It's an exploration in the reinvention of yourself. But I see the stifled artists, doing the same old thing, over and over again. Their style has become their prison. What should be freeing has become habitual behavior often masquerading as original art when originality is what it now lacks the most.

I think the happiest artists continually seek new ground, reinvention, rejuvenation, growth, and to broaden their scope and take on new challenges.

So much so they are just copying themselves. It's as if the staircase and the ascent has ended. Summit-less.

Sometimes if growth within one's chosen craft has stagnated, it's time for another chosen art or artistry. I'm a painter and have been for thirty years. I'm a writer and have been at least since high school. I'll be frank in saying though, more of my growth these days is happening with writing over painting. It's the place I look most for improvement because while both are my creative voices, writing is currently louder with more to say and I don't give it a second thought. I go for it because I want to improve as a writer.

Seeking improvement may take some guidance though. It's often said when you are learning something like tennis and you play with someone better than you, they raise your game. If you are the best at a given skill in the room, while you have the ability to improve others around you, you may not find the need or ability to improve yourself. But sometimes the teacher needs to be taught.

I think the most important key here is your artistic improvement "may" need to jump from one medium to another. A painter may need to become a sculptor. An actor may need to become a director. A dancer may need to become a choreographer. A columnist may need to become a novelist.

In my case, and certainly this is the case with some other artists, I'm multi-artistic. Painting a picture with paint, words, or film is essentially the same and yet quite different. For my 25th career anniversary, I decided I wanted more story depth for my upcoming show, which was a year off. I not only wanted to paint paintings for that celebratory show title, "The Land Beneath My Feet," I wanted to present a broader vision. I thought a book would be a great addition. One that could show many examples of my paintings and also tell my story. So, with the help of my wife Linda, I also created and self-published this book, bearing the same title as my show. But even that wasn't enough. I felt strongly that the show needed to have a more significant visual voice, even more than just creating paintings for sale.

So, I set out to produce, co-shoot, and direct a short film about my story. Though under ten minutes in length, it took almost eleven months to shoot it through all four seasons. My video, also titled, *The Land Beneath My Feet*, can easily be found on YouTube. The experience challenged me to grow artistically, and I felt great about it. I not only told a complete story, but I also did so across several mediums, with little to no creative boundaries. I improved immensely with them all. It was very satisfying.

For me, improvement is a valuable currency, something I can spend or save.

Realized gains in the self-improvement of one's skills are very much a feel-good thing. For me, improvement is a valuable currency, something I can spend or save. It's a measurable wealth and one I hope to continue making sizable deposits into with the years to come. I don't see a time when I will say I've improved enough, all done, *fini*, skill bank is all full. Look at the things you would like to artfully accomplish as a treasure chest and consider the word *improvement* as sacred, and you'll see happiness in your future!

CHAPTER 14

Ageless Artistry!

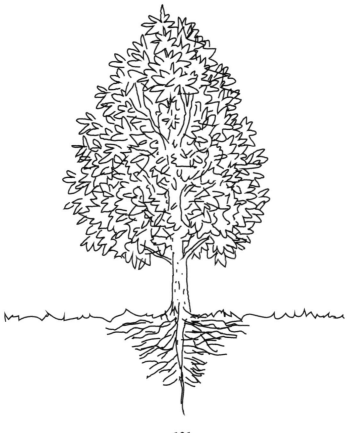

Age is but a number.
Like candles on a cake.
With it comes great wisdom.
And the artful life you make!

ART AND THE AGING. None of us are getting any younger, and in fact, baby boomers are retiring at a rapid rate. Some will play golf, go for walks, and visit with grandchildren. Others will continue working or find endless ways to occupy themselves. Sadly, some will not.

My mother-in-law, who lived in Denver, passed away at the age of ninety-seven. She had lived a pretty full life. She worked into her early eighties, started winding down until ninety when her driving became dangerous and that was that. After giving up driving, her world became rather small. She became one of those that dreamt of simply dying in her home. Then a fall sent her to the hospital, followed by rehabilitation and finally to a retirement home. She never saw the home she planned to die in again. Sad.

But sadder still is that she never planned to properly occupy a still-living mind and trust me, these care facilities don't do a great job of it either. Her knees were shot, but her mind was still working. Days blended into one continuous timeline of same old, same old, which rob us of mental stimulation. It all becomes much like a day in the life of the movie *Groundhog Day.* You wake to the same old thing trying to figure things out, only unlike the movie, you slip more into confusion. Without the responsibility of having to know what day it is and nothing to keep it sharp, life can quickly become a daze. There's nothing to stir the soul.

> *I'm convinced that humans need to be accomplishing things almost right up until the day they die.*

I'm convinced that humans need to be accomplishing things almost right up until the day they die. Without something to conceptualize and follow through to completion, time plays a trick on your mind. You become delusional and confused, and that creates nothing but frustration. We as humans need accomplishment. I'm also convinced that these accomplishments we need require at least some mind and hand coordination. This is where creativity can reign supreme. Usually, the closest activity offered to the aging is bingo or solitaire. Personally, I'd rather just doodle endlessly.

Reading is a great thing, no doubt. But it is not a creative one. Writing is creative. My mother-in-law read, watched movies, and some TV into her old age, but she stopped making things, even meals. The things she did may have occupied time, but not in an effective way. Accomplishing anything was in the past. Keeping a list of tasks and having a schedule really help. But making something and being creative requires imagination, hand-eye coordination, and problem-solving, and delivers both frustration and satisfaction.

The carrot and the stick are what give us a sense of accomplishment and bring value to our lives with the time we have left. I am convinced I could get more health out of these aging minds in one week then the whole industry does in a year. If you have an aging parent and spend time with them, get their brains working. But if you *are* the aging parent, get yours working while you still can.

The other day I was talking to a neighbor walking along the road. He's up in his years now and alone, as his wife passed away several years ago. Several times during our short discussion he used the phrase, "I'm just staring at four walls." Staring at four walls seems like prison terminology. It lacks the mentality of the freedom we all deserve. Your imagination is the key to unlocking yourself mentally. And being creative will never let you see four blank walls for long.

Your imagination is the key to unlocking yourself mentally. And being creative will never let you see four blank walls for long.

Robert Gurtler, the once-mayor of one of our tiny local towns in Northern Virginia, wouldn't mind me saying that he is not a young man. But he most certainly is energetic and youthfully minded. Bob runs marathons like most of us have dinner. He keeps going regardless of his age or his pace on any given day. Crossing the finish line still gives him a sense of accomplishment too, because he does so always winning his age class and dressed in a Batman costume!

Don't call him crazy, call him youthful!

For those of us getting along in years, or who have loved ones who are, simplistic artistic learning can be an excellent medication for the idle mind. Just trying to draw a piece of fruit with pencil on paper can bring that sense of accomplishment. The drive is no longer about money. Just something which requires a bit of a schedule to move forward, helps our brains to work, and allows us to see progress and completion. From that result comes a sense of accomplishment and hopefully, the instinctive desire to accomplish other things. To stay mentally fit, to want to live instead of waiting to die.

Mental fitness can have positive benefits on much younger minds too. I have a client in his fifties. A successful businessman, he comes home from his workday and spends a few hours unwinding while doing intricate, colorful, high piece-count puzzles. It is his brain interacting with his hands, along with having complete control in doing so. Often, work situations and distractions rob us of our ability to complete something. For him, the puzzles allow his mind to find solutions while having fun, but also accomplish a goal by bringing it to completion.

You are most certainly alive until you are dead. So I say, please act accordingly!

The older minds we have today are some of the greatest minds ever. They have endured rigorous hardship, victorious achievements, and they deserve a continued sense of gratitude and accomplishment for their efforts. Even the most elementary creative endeavors can offer true mental growth in a time of weak knees and loss of familiar surroundings. If you or a family member find the days melting together, try to get creative. It's never too late to make something! You are most certainly alive until you are dead. So I say, please act accordingly!

CHAPTER 15

Creating While Listening to Music or Books

Creativity can be one of solitude.
And music the company you keep.
Or an audible book, or podcast,
Will keep you from counting sheep!

I COULD SAY IN studio lingo, that creativity is music to my ears. Studio time is generally one of solitude. Sometimes silence is golden, other times it's not and can bring on a bit of loneliness. I'm also not sure how I would do in a co-op studio situation either, one where chit-chat can flourish. I'm likely as good at chit-chat as anyone—duly noted, but one must remember to keep their eye on the ball, or the brush, as it were.

I've done a little of the book on tape thing over the years, and it depends on the story as to whether I'll keep up with it or mindlessly wander into my painting, where my mind belongs! When I'm painting though, I'm not there to listen to a story. I'm there to create one. Finding myself having to concentrate on another story, then losing myself in my painting, only to have to go back and pick up on something I've missed in the book's audible delivery seems a pointless exercise. Sometimes it works, and sometimes it doesn't. It's as simple as that, and admittedly, I could be guilty of not being able to chew gum and walk at the same time.

I happen to think most artists choose some form of audible companionship over silence, and I personally prefer music.

Multitasking is all fine and good, as long as one of those things isn't really that important. It's like the person texting while walking and walking into a pole or alas, crashing a car. In any event, we all have to find what works for us, and if it assists you in a motivational way, perfect. If not, well then, move along. I happen to think most artists choose some form of audible companionship over silence, and I personally prefer music.

Music just seems to be my company of choice. I used to fire up my iPod and Bose combo, and have at it. But Pandora or Spotify is the new thing, and you may be reading this book sometime in the future and thinking, *those are ancient too!* In any event, most songs are only a few minutes long, which is harder to get wrapped up into than a multi-chapter story. So, I push the button, find a playlist or shuffle it up, and let it flow. Like books, music is also artful and a language all its own. It's a good fit, but it has to fit you!

As you well know, there's a wide variety of music out there. To be frank, there's little of it that I don't have some interest in. That said, some of you reading along may have this romantic picture of every artist listening to Mozart, as he or she whimsically paints the stem of a rose. Maybe opera or holy chants of some sort come to mind? It all has its glorious place in the grand creative scheme of things. But for some, often myself included, these genres can be a little too melodic, long-winded, and of slow energy.

I listen to a bit of everything. I've even listened to marching hymns, which are great fun. Maybe too much so, as I find myself parading around the studio twirling my brush like a baton and not painting. It's just not a pretty picture.

Past this account of things, I do indeed listen to every-thing else. Rock, country, blues, pop, country rock, show tunes, jazz, reggae, folk, R&B, Motown, new age, instru-mental, guitar (I play a bit too), Latin, a little hip-hop, even some metal. My library looks like ten people of all different ages are sharing it, and it covers music from about the 1930s forward, though the last thirty years get the most airtime. I can go from Ella to Al Green in a minute!

Sometimes it's just jazz or even country, but the music needs to be in sync with me and me with it. It has to be a good fit. Admittedly, I most often just throw it all at myself. That is to say, while I do have some playlists which can funnel moods or interests, for the most part, I just let it happen and see what comes up. Shuffle me. Ever heard Chet Atkins, Al Green, Zeppelin, Bob Dylan and Diana Krall, all in a row? How about Bob Marley, John 5, B.B. King, Joan Osborne, and then Jack Mack and the Heart Attacks? The silliness goes on and on, but welcome to my world. I *live an artful life,* and music, and the good vibes it brings, are an essential part of it!

For me, songs are just programmable energy levels.

For me, songs are just programmable energy levels. Some are story driven, some more era-focused, and others are all about the beat. The best part of it is, I find that the music I play never lets my energy go flat. I'm going along creatively doing my thing and just when I mindlessly think I'm at a pace, the pace changes. It's the immediacy of being in a zone and all of a sudden hearing the howls and beat of Michael Jackson's *Thriller* grabbing you. Who needs caffeine? And afterward, Jackson Brown comes in and brings my heart rate back down, only to have Joe Cocker covering a Beatle's tune lift it back up again. I love it, and so does my creativity.

Now with my writing, I have found that music doesn't assist in this process. Being moderately dyslexic is challenge enough. My typing is like a minefield of typo-bombed words that challenge the limits of spellcheck. I get by, but music would only prolong the ending. Heck, maybe I should have just been a musician!

But I have spoken to authors who need to be in a busy coffee shop with their laptop while listening to music with earphones before they can really get into writing. WHAT? I can hardly imagine, or maybe I can. As painters, these same people might have to be in a quiet studio with nobody and no music. We're creatures of habit, and the moral to this story is to find what habits fit your creativity. This is all about you!

I will say this; fuel for your rocket is a must, and one person's thrust can be another person's fire.

I will say this; fuel for your rocket is a must, and one person's thrust can be another person's fire. While creating, you want the things around you to be in line with your intentions and to fuel the inner you!

CHAPTER 16

Some Artful Ways to Get Started

There's no shortage
Of creative things to try.
Have a look at this starter list.
Your limit is the sky!

THERE ARE SEEMINGLY ENDLESS ways to *Live An Artful Life*, just as there are endless ways to have fun with creativity! So, for fun, I've listed a few—maybe a few of your favorites! I'm sure there's something there for you, and you won't hurt my feelings a bit if you add to the list!

- Decorating for the holidays.
- Taking a painting class.
- Learning a musical instrument.
- Taking a cooking class.
- Setting a beautiful dinner table.
- Serving a meal aesthetically.
- Redesigning a room in your home.
- Helping a friend change up a room in his or her home.
- Making a scrapbook.
- Doodling.
- Sketching.
- Making a flower arrangement.
- Designing a small garden area.
- Making a wreath for your door.

- Setting up your closet by color or pattern.
- Purchasing a complete outfit.
- Purchasing a three-day outfit ensemble.
- Painting kitchen cabinets.
- Getting a tattoo.
- Designing a tattoo.
- Taking a poetry class.
- Going to an art museum.
- Attending an art opening or First Friday.
- Visiting an artist's studio.
- Purchasing a piece of art.
- Attending a local play.
- Attending a recital.
- Helping make costumes for a school play.
- Volunteering to make sets for a local or school play.
- Videotaping yourself singing a song on your smartphone.
- Hand-making a birthday card for a friend.
- Donating to an arts organization.
- Seeing live music.
- Having live music in your home.
- Going to a concert.
- Making a small sculpture from clay.
- Making jewelry.
- Dying silk.
- Tie-dying a tee shirt.
- Custom painting a car.
- Drawing anything.
- Taking photographs.

- Making short films.
- Building scale models.
- Writing poetry.
- Writing short stories.
- Writing a book.
- Writing letters to friends.
- Doing crafts.
- Attending a paint-and-sip.
- Reading an art history book.
- Tying scarves in new ways.
- Accessorizing your home or a friend's home.
- Configuring a new car.
- Choosing colors to paint a room.
- Choosing a beautiful photo frame.
- Buying flowers for yourself.
- Buying flowers for a friend.
- Attending a fashion show.
- Helping a child with an art project.
- Doing art with your children.
- Dancing the night away.
- Taking a dancing class.
- Dancing while making dinner.
- Going to the ballet.
- Going to see modern dance.
- Volunteering at a music therapy organization.
- Supporting the arts through a donation.
- Coloring in a coloring book.
- Doing a puzzle.
- Giving a puzzle.
- Visiting a botanical garden.

- Watching a movie.
- Reading a book then watching the movie made from the book.
- Joining a book club.
- Learning a new language.
- Helping others learn your language.
- Learning about the art of other cultures.
- Learning art terminology.
- Attending a poetry reading.
- Watching a sunset.
- Watching a sunrise.
- Taking photos of a sunrise or sunset and posting them on social media.
- Hosting an art show.
- Posting photos on Instagram.
- Making porcelain.
- Creating balloon figures.
- Decorating.
- Going to an art fair.
- Joining a gardening club.
- Commissioning a painting.
- Attending an artist's lecture.
- Auditioning for a play.
- Taking a cake decorating class.
- Decorating a cake.
- Making seasonal or holiday cookies.
- Taking voice lessons.
- Designing a cartoon.
- Playing with an art app on your tablet.

CHAPTER 17

Final Thoughts

Seek a carefree life!
Seek creativity!
Let your imagination inspire you!
And live life artfully!

I CANNOT SAY ENOUGH about the blessings creativity has brought me. I hope in the greatest way that this book verbalizes that message loud and clear, and offers you new possibilities, or validates a way of life you have already discovered. Being creative is healthy, both physically and mentally. It allows your brain to think freely and for your body to be personally productive. Your creative output is entirely up to you. It is not only under your power; it is within your power. Best of all is the message of how some form of creativity is for everyone, from the artist to the patron of the arts.

For all of us, my deepest message is to be carefree. Not care*less*, but carefree! In my opinion, creativity is a stress reliever, but we as humans certainly can make anything stressful. The key is to find happiness and let your creative juices flow out of you, not back at you like a fire hose dousing your internal flame or your burning desire to have fun. Being creative is outward. Appreciated creativity is inward. If you live an artful life, you understand this.

If you do not want to call yourself an artist, trust me, it's no problem. If you do not feel a draw toward creativity, but you find yourself in love with and in support of the creativity of others around you, believe me when I say, the art world loves you! You live an artful life as much as any artist, and simply surrounding yourself with creativity will be of great benefit to you. With all honesty, though, my guess is if you have surrounded yourself with creativity or creative types, you are more creative than you recognize. I've never met anyone who isn't creative, but I've met many who don't see this in themselves.

I wanted to create this book in a way where once read, it would allow the reader to quickly refresh themselves by merely flipping through the title chapters and re-reading the enlarged text phrases. This can be done in a matter of minutes, and if any one of those phrases jumps off the page, it's a sign that more time should be spent in this area of the book. If you find an area of this book of particular importance, bookmark it, visit it and grow. Here are a few of my favorite words to you.

Life is a journey and living artfully can make this journey more fun, more interesting, even more bearable for some.

———

To live an artful life is to immerse yourself in something other than the mundane and enjoy life to its fullest through a world of visionary exploration.

———

After all, a great life is not measured by how old you become, it is measured by how young you feel while aging.

———

Carefreeness is about happiness, carelessness is the opposite, and carefulness lacks intelligence.

———

To live an artful life, you need to refocus yourself on the greatness around you

Acknowledgments

THROUGH EACH CREATIVE ENDEAVOR I have enjoyed, my loving wife Linda has been at my side with not only complete support, but collaboration. I cannot thank or credit her enough. A talented artist in her own right, Linda has excellent attention for detail, sound judgment, and a motivated attitude. We live an artful life together.

I must also make mention of our cat Revlon, who along with her dearly departed sister Maybelline, offered thousands of hours of devoted support, often dozing on the desk between my keyboard and screen.

Editor Christin Perry, supportive friend, graphic artist, and editor Clair Hendrix, along with designer Glen Edelstein, all have played very important contributive parts in having this book become a reality, and we thank and appreciate them for doing so.

Family and friends are the best, but I must truly give thanks to each person who confided in me for guidance. Each allowed me to help formulate *Live An Artful Life* into a book for people of all ages to enjoy.

About The Author

TOM NEEL IS AN accomplished artist, writer, photographer, designer, and art show judge, living in Virginia. Along with his thirty plus years as a fine art painter, his artful life has been complemented by gallery ownership, creative consulting and public speaking.

Imagination never dwindled throughout his childhood, but his early love of automobiles became his first career which grew to a national sales manager position while living in Los Angles in the mid-1980s. This time in his life certainly aided in developing his business sense, which he attributes in part, to his success as an artist. But that time was also key in having him understand something essential about himself. That deep within, his calling was creativity. He decided to live his dream of becoming an artist, and his life-changing fine art career was born.

With over 40 one man shows, and financial fine art success to his credit, Tom Neel's tranquil, scenic paintings primarily of Virginia, are the part of many private and corporate collections, both here and abroad. His commissions vary widely in subject matter.

Along with his art career, Tom and his wife Linda founded Live An Artful Life ® in 2008. This was not only the name for their art gallery; the name additionally encompassed their inspirational website and their active way of life. He also created a newspaper column called The Artist's Perspective, offering creative advice and his artful life philosophy. During this time, Tom spoke with hundreds of gallery customers, his art commission clients, and children through his work with schools and including those labeled with disabilities, and their parents. Tom came to understand that many suffered what he felt was creative starvation and that the appreciation for creativity and the arts could be life-changing. He feels his greatest gift is sharing how to *Live An Artful Life.*

CPSIA information can be obtained
at www.ICGtesting.com
Printed in the USA
FFHW021110070219
50463407-55678FF